Compromised Christianity

"I Don't Want To Be A Half-Meassured Christian."

Michael McAllister

Relentless Intl Ministries

ISBN: 979-8-9904144-0-2

E-BOOK ISBN: 979-8-9904144-1-9

COMPROMISED CHRISTIANITY

Contents

Dedication

This book is dedicated to my beautiful wife, Sydni, our daughter Aria, and all our children to come. I love you so much and am so thankful to be blessed by you. To be called your husband, father, and friend.

To my children, always chase your dreams. Don't let them sit on the shelf waiting for it to come to you because it won't. Chase it! I believe in you!

Acknowledgments

I must start this off first acknowledging my Lord and Savior, Jesus Christ. Without you Lord, I would not be here to write this book and share the words that you have given me. I am so thankful to everyone who has poured into me and into this book these past few years. My amazing wife, Sydni, thank you for always believing in me and being the woman of God that you are for me, your family, and your children.

To our mothers, Julie, and Lisa, for their never-ending love and support. Both of you are a rock for us to stand on, lean on, and cry on. This book could not have come to fruition without either of you. The support you give, in every single way, will never be taken for granted or forgotten. I love you so much!

To my brothers, Matthew, and Brandon, thank you for helping me bring this dream to life. Your investment in me has made this possible. Thank you. To my friend and sister, Crystal, I can't thank you enough for all that you have done for me during the process of writing this. Your support means the world to me. To all of my family, thank you all for your love and support. JohnJames Emmino, thank you so much for your incredible investment in me and this book. Your blessing helped in such an amazing. Thank you, and I pray God blesses you more than you could think.

Pastor Jason Creech, thank you for all of the mentoring and conversations you have given me. You made a big impact on me and helped bring this book together. To the Schatzline family (Pat, Karen, Nate, and Abby), you became family to me the moment Nate and I became friends in seventh grade. Thank you all for the impact you had on me in some of the roughest and worst seasons of my life and continue to make. I can honestly say that my life has been shaped by all of you. Lastly, I would like to thank my editor, Caitlin Miller, you have transformed this manuscript into a work of art! You are amazing at what you do, and I look forward to working with you again.

Thank you to everyone for all that you do and have done for me, and for my family. I pray that this book will become, exceed, and multiply even more than what we are believing for. I am forever grateful for all of you!

Foreword

By Pat Schatzline

"A voice of one Crying out in the Wilderness"

This book is a compass for those who are ready to experience intimacy and passion at a whole new level with Jesus! As I read, "Compromised Christianity" from my dear son in the faith, Author Michael McAllister, I heard the Lord say, "Michael is a voice of one crying out in the wilderness." I truly believe that this book is a clarion call to awaken to next level faith. From the beginning to the end, this book will set you aflame for more of Jesus.

First, let me share about the Author. I have had the honor of knowing Michael most of his life. God allowed us to help steward his life beginning in his junior high years. I have watched him grow into a man of purity and purpose. His story is one that will be revealed in later books, but I will just say that he is one of the greatest overcomers I have ever met. He faced many obstacles and crossroads that were sent by the enemy to derail his destiny, but JESUS! When you read this powerful book, it is important to realize that the author writes this book from a place of brokenness that was produced in the furnace of affliction and the altar of restoration. Michael is a walking testimony of freedom! You will read accounts of Michael's life in this book that will make you sit up and say, "If he can, then I can."

In his book, "Compromised Christianity", Michael confronts with incredible grace the traps of being a lukewarm believer. He exposes the reader to the danger of "having a form of godliness but denying its power" (2 Tim. 3:5). This book will set your heart aflame as you begin to realize all that God has for you. As you read this book you will experience moments where you must lay the book down and crawl into the place of encounter. Prepare for your faith to be awakened!

Here are a few spiritual shifts that will happen as you read "Compromised Christianity":

- Your hunger for the word of God will increase as Michael shares the beauty of the reflection of change that takes place as you read God's Word.

- Your passion to help rescue the lost with the Love of God will increase 100-fold.

- Your private worship will manifest in a public way. The opinions of others will no longer influence you as you cry out for more of Jesus.

- The reflection in the mirror will no longer reflect a self-consumed person, but rather a reflection of the Savior who died for all. The brokenness in you will remind others that you have encountered something greater than your past.

- For those passionate about Jesus who do not feel like they fit into today's Christianity, this book will be the answer you have so longingly desired to experience. In other words, this book is for what I call, "The orphans of revival." These are those who once experienced the depth of freedom in Christ but seem to have misplaced it.

- You will learn the power of guarding your heart from the enemies' schemes and plans. God has called you out of darkness into His marvelous light (1 Peter 2:9).

- You will decide to become a "Mobile-upper room." God has placed His Spirit in you for the greater works.

- For those that feel as though freedom is so far out of your reach then I implore you to read this quote from this book, "Can

> I tell you something? When our shields are heavily damaged from battle, they can always be mended and welded back to full strength and even stronger. Our faith is built and made stronger in our place of prayer."

Finally, I must say that this book was written for all generations. It is for the young and the old. It is for the lost and the found. In other words, it is for you! Give this book to everyone you know.

Pat Schatzline
Author, Evangelist, and CEO
Remnant Ministries Int'l

Introduction

I was praising and worshiping God at home a few years ago when the Holy Spirit first spoke this book to me. I was so excited and terrified at the same time. I have never had the desire to do anything like this before. As a matter of fact, I have never even liked reading! When the Holy Spirit put this book in my heart, I said, "Are you sure? Are you sure you picked the right guy?"

I asked that because I don't have the best vocabulary or the highest reading levels. English and writing were always my least favorite subjects. Why would God want to use me to write a book? Surely there is someone more suited than me to write a book. I have come to learn, though, that God chooses those who are labeled "unqualified" to do His work so that there is no doubt that it comes from Him. The Bible tells us that before the earth's foundations were even laid, God had a plan and purpose for each of us.

I love Paul's words in *1 Corinthians 2:1-3 NIV* "And so it was with me brothers and sisters. When I came to you, I did not come with eloquence or human wisdom as I proclaimed to you the testimony about God. For I resolved to know nothing while I was with you except Jesus Christ and Him crucified. I came to you in weakness and with great fear and trembling. My message and my preaching were not with wise and persuasive words, but with a demonstration of the Spirit's power, so that your faith might not rest on human wisdom, but on God's power."

I write this book purely by the guidance and leading of God's Holy Spirit. I know that I am not the most qualified person to write a book; but my spiritual Father, Pat Schatzline, has always said, "God doesn't always call the qualified, but He always qualifies the called."

This book is for the modern Christian, those who proclaim to be believers but live without Christ in their life; the many who say they believe but live far from the cross. Christians in today's culture have decided that it's okay for them to pick and choose what parts of the Bible they want to believe and not believe in. The identity of being a Christian has become so distorted that we can say we are Christian and not even know Jesus. We have become so quick to blame God when things go wrong and become angry with Him and then not give glory, thanks, or praise when things go right.

The Cambridge Dictionary defines compromise as this: "to allow your principles to be less strong or your standards or morals to be lower." One translation in Hebrew for compromise is "half measured." I don't know about you, but I don't want to be a half-measured Christian!

I'm afraid modern-day Christians have lost sight of the true meaning of Christianity. The definition of a Christian in the Cambridge dictionary is "someone who believes and follows the teachings of Christ." To be a Christian is to be a follower of Christ; we all know that already.

I love to do word searches and find their definitions because it ties the meaning of things in an even tighter knot! What am I trying to get at? Stick with me for a second, and you'll see what I'm getting at. To be a Christian is to be a follower of Christ, right? According to Cambridge, one of the definitions of a follower is "someone who obeys or supports a person or that person's ideas."

Now, let's put all of that together. A Christian is someone who believes in Jesus and follows Jesus by obeying His teachings and supporting the Kingdom of Heaven! Being a Christian is so much more than praying a prayer one time. It is a *daily* commitment to reading the Word of God and being obedient to its teachings, to be a disciple of Jesus and exemplify Him in all we do!

A few times at my job, someone has approached me and said, "Thank you for being the Christian that you are. Simply watching how you live has set an example to me and made me want to change." A few months later, one of those colleagues told me he gave his heart to Jesus and asked me if I would come to his water baptism. I'm not trying to boast by sharing this story; all the credit goes to Jesus for helping him make that decision. However, if I had been living like some people do—as a half-measured Christian—my colleague might have been even more turned away from God.

This book, I pray, will provide light into a dark world. That it will serve as a map to living a Christ-like life and being set free from the world's view of Christianity. I hope and pray that the Holy Spirit uses me to speak to the hearts of all who read.

Furthermore, I want everyone to know that there is no condemnation in the Kingdom of Heaven; Romans 8 says it beautifully. If you are reading this, know there is no shaming, guilt-tripping, or anything else. This book is to lead the way for God to bring restoration and healing! The enemy will try his best to make you feel condemnation, but that is not the case. There will be Holy Spirit conviction, but never condemnation. God loves you so much and wants you to live in His fullness. I pray that this will help lead you there!

I want to pray over you before you begin this journey.

"Heavenly Father, I thank you for this child of yours! I thank you for the life that you have given them. Lord, I pray for guidance as they read this book that you have spoken through

me, that your Holy Spirit may speak and take the lead. Father, I pray for blessings and your peace that surpasses all understanding. I proclaim and declare a hedge of protection over the enemy's attacks right now in the name of Jesus! Father, guard our hearts and ears as we embark on this journey. Let us equip the whole armor of you so that only your words and your Spirit may pierce our hearts. I thank you, Father, for loving us and wanting us to live in the fullness of your blessing and Spirit in this life. I ask, Lord, that you take the lead and let us truly follow you in all we do. Open the ears to our hearts and let your Spirit speak. Let these words penetrate and resonate in our hearts so that we can get back to the place where we belong, and you be in the center of it all. In Jesus' mighty name. Amen!"

CHAPTER 1
The Conformed Christian

"You are either in the Word, and the Word is conforming you to the image of Jesus Christ, or you are in the world, and the world is squeezing you into its mold. -Howard G. Hendricks "

What does it mean to be a conformed Christian? I believe that is a straightforward question to answer. A conformed Christian is someone who proclaims to be a follower of Jesus but is also one who is in harmony with the ways of this world. The Bible mentions on multiple occasions that we are to set ourselves apart from the world, yet we try to live on both sides of the fence. Another way to describe a conformed Christian is a compromised Christian. According to the Cambridge Dictionary, compromise means to allow your principles to be less strong or your standards or morals to be lower. Wow! What a powerful and gut-punching statement. As Christians, we are supposed to be set apart and be light shining into a dark world, but I am afraid we have become a match trying to light a stadium.

One translation in Hebrew for compromise is "half measured." Have we become half-measured Christians going to church on Sundays but living un-Christ-like Monday through Saturday? I know that I have. I have proclaimed Jesus and how great He is, but then turned around and lived how I wanted to.

Let me tell you a little bit about my story.

I grew up going to a small church right outside Birmingham, Alabama. The kind where everyone knew everyone and their momma, brother, and sister. I grew up hearing all the stories and sermons *about* Jesus, but I never really knew *who* Jesus was. Back in middle school, I met my friend Nate, and we quickly became like brothers. His father was an evangelist, and they invited me to a youth conference he was scheduled to speak at. It was in a moment during the altar call that I met Jesus for the first time, and my life changed forever. I became on fire for God and knew that He was calling me to ministry, and that was what I would do.

Now, let's fast forward a few years. In high school, I was introduced to the party lifestyle and all that came with it – drugs, alcohol and you name it. I got a taste of the world and what it had to offer. I quickly stopped going to church, left all my godly friends behind, and began to drive myself into a long battle of compromise and conformity. I got so deep into that lifestyle, so lost that I couldn't even recognize myself in the mirror. In fact, when I looked at my reflection, I was disgusted with myself and couldn't believe the man I had become.

I was once so strong in my faith, knowing exactly who I was in Christ, but now conformed and molded to the ways of this world. Alright, let's fast forward a few more years. I am twenty-two and being admitted into a rehab facility. Now, I know that doesn't seem like anything to be excited about, but let me tell you how glorious it was! It was a revival of my soul and spirit for four months straight.

The facility I was in was led by some of the most remarkable men of God I have ever met. They led all of us guys in that center to more than just sobriety; they led us out of captivity by the power of Jesus and His Holy Spirit. It was a place ignited by the fire of God where I rediscovered my true identity and purpose in Christ. Romans 12:2 has been such a key Scripture in my life ever since because that was me—conformed to the ways of the world but now I am transformed because I was made new in Christ!

I love how the Amplified version says it:

> "And do not be conformed to this world [any longer with its superficial values and customs], but be trans-

> formed *and* progressively changed [as you mature spiritually] by the renewing of your mind [focusing on godly values and ethical attitudes], so that you may prove [for yourselves] what the will of God is, that which is good and acceptable and perfect [in His plan and purpose for you]."

The Word of God is so powerful. I love that verse so much. I was once blind and walking astray, but God loved me so much that He turned me around and transformed me from the inside out. That's why this verse is so powerful: we are transformed by the renewing of our minds by reading and studying the Word of God! When we study God's Word, it is more than just reading a book. (We will get more into that in the coming chapters, though.)

> "He that would be conformed to Christ's image, and become a Christ-like man, must be constantly studying Christ Himself." -J.C Ryle

One question I have asked myself many times is, how did I let myself get there? Knowing what I know now, it becomes clear to me. I began to do things that I shouldn't have done, which led to the enemy having a foothold in my faith. The enemy tried to take away my identity in Christ and deceive my perception of Him.

Let's look deeper into what it means to live as a compromised Christian. The Word 'deceived' means to cause (someone) to believe something that is not true, typically to gain some kind of personal advantage; failing to admit to oneself that something is true (of a thing) gives a mistaken impression. 'Perception' is the ability to see, hear, or become aware of something through the senses; a way of regarding, understanding, or interpreting something. Also, a few definitions in Hebrew are the following: seizure, capture, grasp, outlook, and hold.

The enemy wants to do his absolute best to deceive our perception of ourselves. He is a master liar and deceiver. Putting these definitions together, this is what speaks to me. In our outlook as Christians today, our perceptions of what it means to be a follower of Christ have been distorted. We claim Jesus, but we stunt our growth and walk in Christ because we have trouble believing that everything we read in the Bible is true. Or maybe we have put our trust into someone who has given us a wrong impression of what a true disciple of Christ looks like.

Also, we have the devil who is constantly whispering in our ears. "That it isn't true," he says. "You don't have to believe all of that." He does that to gain personal advantage or leverage over us. If he can deceive our perception and we start to believe it, then the way we see ourselves and our regard and understating of God and His love for us can begin to slip. That is why it is so important to know who our Father is and who we are in Him! Otherwise, compromise will slowly begin to bring us down.

I have learned that it isn't always like a wrecking ball taking massive chunks or an entire wall down in one blow; no, it is a slow storm that weakens the mortar holding the bricks together. It is the little doubts and attacks taking them down one by one, and before you know it, the wall is down enough for the enemy to get you right where he wants you. The Bible tells us that the devil stalks like a lion waiting to pounce on you. The devil is here to steal, to kill, and to destroy. If he can get your walls down just enough to pounce on you, that is exactly what he will try to do. So, how do we keep the enemy from deceiving us and keep our perceptions true? Well, I am glad that you asked We do this by reaffirming who we are in Christ!

> "The more you reaffirm who you are in Christ, the more your behavior will begin to reflect your true identity."
> -Neil T. Anderson.

I love what Neil T. Anderson says in the quote above. The more we know and walk in who we are in Christ, the more we will be able to resist the devil and not be deceived by his lies. Our best way to no longer be a conformed Christian is to know our Identity in Christ. Avoid the Identity Crisis!

> "If our identity is in our work, rather than Christ, success will go to our heads, and failure will go to our hearts." -Timothy Keller.

As I mentioned in the book's intro, I love to look up words and break down their meanings. So, let's break down Identity Crisis. One definition of identity is "the distinguishing character or personality of an individual" or "the individual characteristics by which a thing or person is recognized or known." Another definition in Hebrew is "oneness."

A crisis is a difficult or dangerous situation that needs serious attention, a paroxysmal attack of pain, distress, or disordered function. The Word paroxysmal comes from the Greek Word *paroxynein*, meaning to stimulate.

The enemy wants to steal your identity in Christ so that he can take the distinguishing character (or your oneness) with God. Doing so puts you in a dangerous place where the enemy can make constant attacks, stimulating pain and distress, manipulating you into thinking you are worthless, and deceiving your perception of God and your value.

The devil wants you to feel worthless and unvalued. John 10:10 tells us that he is here to steal, kill, and destroy. If the enemy can steal your identity, he will kill your self-worth and try to destroy you from within.

It is so important that we know exactly who we are in Christ. So that we can put on the full armor of God, and any attack the enemy throws at us will fall short. You are a child of the most High God! The King of Kings, the Prince of Peace, and the Great I AM! You are worthy in every area you think you fall short. The first step in living a faith-filled life is taking back your identity!

> "Yet to all who did receive him, to those who believed in his name, he gave the right to become children of God."
> John 1:12 NIV

I love this quote from Howard G. Hendricks that I read: "There was no identity crisis in the life of Jesus Christ. He knew who He was. He knew where He had come from and why he was here. And he knew where He was going. And when you are that liberated, then you can serve."

Jesus was tried by the devil more than we will ever be, but He knew who He was—the Son of God! Jesus walked in power and authority of that knowledge without doubt or hesitation. When Jesus rose again after being crucified and went into Heaven, He left us with the gift of the Holy Spirit so that we could walk in His likeness. He gave us the power and ability to trample the serpent beneath our feet. It's time for you to stand up in the authority that Jesus gave you and take back what is yours!

I want you to lift your hands and pray this with me. Declare these words with authority!

"Jesus! Jesus, I need you; forgive me for my sins, Lord. I don't want to live a compromised life. I want the fullness of you! Let your heavens roar over me right now. In the mighty name of Jesus Christ, I declare that what the enemy has taken from me be let loose right now! I am taking back my authority and my identity in Jesus' name! I am a child of God, the King of Kings, and Lord of Lords. Devil, I command you to let loose right now, in Jesus' name! From this moment forward, I choose to live and walk as Jesus has saved me to live! No more compromise, no more deception, and no more identity crisis in the mighty name of Jesus!"

AMEN!!

Welcome to a beautiful journey of fullness in Christ! This journey will still have its difficulties and trials, but I pray as you read, you will be equipped with the tools necessary to move forward. We will be knocked down occasionally, but we never have to go back. I've always loved to use this analogy: imagine you're in a baseball game. You hit the ball and take off running, hoping to make it to base or home plate. You go round first but trip and fall. You don't go back to home plate, so you get up and keep running bases.

Life hits us all in our own ways, but always get up and keep going! With your newfound hope in deepening your walk with God and identity, always remember that God has saved you, and you are HIS! You don't have to go back to what it was before. Life has thrown me many curve balls and even struck me out a time or two, but I remind myself who I am and whose I am: I am God's beloved! I have been sober since October 2014 and have never gone back to who I used to be. I was once full of compromise and conformity, but now I am full of grace and God's never-ending love!

> "In him we have redemption through his blood, the forgiveness of sins, in accordance with the riches of God's grace." Ephesians 1:7 NIV

> "Since then, you have been raised with Christ, set your hearts on things above, where Christ is, seated at the right hand of God. Set your minds on things above, not on earthly things. For you died, and your life is now hid-

den with Christ in God." Colossians 3:1-3 NIV

CHAPTER 2

Walking Without God's Word & Living Apart from It

"If we want to know the Glory of God, if we want to experience the beauty of God, and if we want to be used by the hand of God, then we must LIVE in the WORD of God." - David Platt

In my walk with God, I have repeatedly realized that I have allowed compromise in an essential part of my life in Christ by walking without God's Word being a significant part or influence of my life and living apart from it.

God's Word, the Bible, has a significant role in the daily lives of a follower of Jesus. As we have already learned, being a faithful Christian and follower of Jesus is obeying and following Jesus' teachings and commandments. We cannot be in His fullness without reading and studying the scriptures. Reading and studying the Bible is like a feeding tube directly flowing from Heaven: if we are not plugged in and being fed all that the Bible has to offer us, then we will become malnourished Christians whose spiritual bones become brittle and easily broken.

When Jesus was in the wilderness fasting and being tempted by the enemy, Jesus quoted the Scripture and said, "No! The Scriptures say, 'People do not live by bread alone, but by every Word that comes from the mouth of God.'" (Matthew 4:4 NLT)

Jesus studied and knew His Father's words. This teaches us a very powerful lesson in the authority and life that God's Word brings us. If Jesus had not been filled with the knowledge of His Father's Word, His time of testing in the wilderness could have had a very different ending. However, Jesus knew who He was and whose He was. He knew that the words of His Father hidden in His heart would sustain Him and nourish Him to resist the devil. Every time Jesus was tempted in the wilderness, He countered the attacks with "No, the Scripture says..." His armor was His Father's Words.

> "Take the helmet of salvation and the sword of the Spirit, which is the word of God." -Eph. 6:17 NIV

Reading and studying the scriptures is essential for us as believers. Hebrews 4 tells us that the Word of God is alive and active, sharper than any double-edged sword. I have always said that the Word of God can only be a double-edged sword if it is open. If the Word is closed, then it is only a single-edge sword, and our battleground becomes more challenging to defend and vulnerable to attacks.

The Bible can supply us with many spiritual benefits, equipping us to fight against our enemy, who lurks like a lion, ready to pounce. Our armor to defend ourselves and the Kingdom of God from the attacks from the enemy is held together with the Word. Reading the Bible has more to offer than spiritual benefits. There are mental, emotional, and even physical benefits to reading the Bible.

Reading and studying the scriptures has helped me in many ways. It helps me to hear from God more clearly and keeps me in check with my spirituality and growth. It has even helped me with quitting addictions. When I went into rehab, I was addicted to alcohol, drugs, and smoking cigarettes. When I first arrived at the facility, I noticed that the program did allow us to smoke and use tobacco to my surprise. I had given up on drugs and alcohol at this point for good, but giving up tobacco was much more complicated than I thought it would be.

I was about a month and a half into the program and was at a point in my spiritual growth where

I wanted to be done with it all for good. My attempts were unsuccessful. I tried using other forms of tobacco to soothe my cravings, but that would only help for just a day or two before I was begging someone for a cigarette. I was praying and asking God to help me break this cycle, and the Holy Spirit spoke to me, "Read the Bible." I sat up and said, "Really, I already do that more ever."

After another day or two, what God was saying to me finally clicked. Whenever I would get the urge or cravings to smoke or use any form of tobacco, I would go into the library and read the Word of God. It wasn't an immediate release, but it was close to it! I'd smoked a pack or two a day for the past six years, but God was working on me in an amazing way. God was filling that urge to smoke and replacing it with a desire to read His Word. It was filling a void that I was trying to fill in my own power, but it was only by the power of God and His Word that I have been tobacco-free since 2014 with no urges or desires.

It was the same with drugs and alcohol. I would drink or take whatever I could get my hands on to fill that empty void inside. It is only by the power and authority of God that I am free from all those addictions, and those voids are filled. I can honestly say that since I graduated from the program on February 1, 2015, there has been no desire, urge, or want to indulge in any of those things. I do not believe in the saying, "Once an addict, always an addict." I believe in this: "I was once an addict, BUT GOD has set me free, and I am no longer in want or need." That is a powerful statement, and I gladly accept that it goes against the status quo.

Scientific studies and research on the benefits of reading Scripture.

I read an article about how reading the Bible affects the brain. In a study conducted by a Harvard Neuroscientist, the researchers scanned and studied the brains of individuals while praying and reading the Scripture. Here are some of their findings:

> "In this study, it was found that there were three regions of the brain that were the most active during these times. Areas such as the frontal attention lobe, the medial prefrontal cortex, and the nucleus accumbens all experience significant increases of activity and responsiveness during religious activities."

> "It was found that high amounts of dopamine were released through the body while reading the Bible. When dopamine is released, you are likely to

> be more focused, motivated, and happy."

> "Reading the Bible can affect neural pathways in the brain. These pathways are in charge of cognitive thinking and behavior. As you read, dopamine releases and affects the thoughts you have while reading the Bible. These factors contribute to changing your ideals and key beliefs."

Dopamine is a "feel good" chemical that our brain releases into our body. It is a neurotransmitter sending messages to all the nerve cells in our body. When dopamine runs through our veins while we read the Word of God, it can stir a whole pot of feel-good emotions about the Bible and what it is doing to our minds.

As we know, our emotions tend to control our thoughts. I tend to have more negative thoughts if I am in negative emotions. However, my thoughts tend to be more positive if I am in good and positive emotions. When I am not in the Word like I should be, my thoughts tend to slide more to the worldly side than the godly.

In an article published by *Christianity Today*, Nicole Martin, executive director of trauma healing at the American Bible Society (ABS), wanted to meet a need and teach people they can find healing to their trauma by reading and studying Scripture. These are some of their findings from this study:

> "A recent ABS-commissioned study by Baylor University, researchers found that combining education about mental health best practices with Bible reading can have a significant benefit. In their study, this reduced the symptoms of post-traumatic stress disorder and increased forgiveness, compassion, and sense of purpose."

That is incredible! Here are some more of their findings to go even deeper:

> "The study showed that the group that went through the program saw a drop in feelings of depression, anxiety, and anger, along with 'complicated grief,' which includes denial of traumatic events, negative affect, and avoiding activities associated with trauma. They also had less depression and fewer suicidal thoughts"

> "...the people in the study experienced an increase in feelings of forgiveness and compassion and reported increased rates of resiliency."

As someone who has dealt with a lot of those feelings associated with trauma, I can stand behind this study. Isn't it amazing how incredible reading the Word of God can affect us in such a positive way? Just as reading the Word of God can have such a tremendous outcome, so can living apart from it.

Not reading the Word and its consequences.

In my journey through life, there have been several seasons when I was not in the Word like I should be. Life can get busy; I understand that better than anyone. There was a season not too long ago that used to keep me out of the Bible. My wife and I welcomed our beautiful baby girl into this world, and life got busy! My wife dreamed of being a stay-at-home mommy and raising our daughter. I was working two jobs while coming home to Daddy duties. I mean it when I said life got busy. We were always tired, wrestling to change diapers and fit in bath time. I went several months without opening my Bible and spending time with God.

There have been other seasons where I was just a lazy Christian. In those seasons, I faced the consequences of living apart from God's Word—consequences like not hearing from God as clearly and slowly drifting away from Him. My faith would decrease, and my prayer life would fade away. It kept me from being the husband, father, and spiritual leader I needed to be.

> "Like newborn babies, you must crave pure spiritual milk so that you will grow into a full experience of salvation. Cry out for this nourishment, now that you have had a taste of the Lord's kindness." -1 Peter 2:2-3 NLT

When we are not in the Word of God, we are not living by God's instructions. Living apart from God's Word leads to the hardening of the heart. Living without the consumption of the living and breathing Word of God can lead to a spiritually dead Christian. Our views on certain things can become blurry; there are no longer definite lines that separate us from the rest of the world. We can become dry and easily offended, brittle, and easy to break because we have lost the nourishment that the Word brings us.

Dig deeper into God's Word.

Have you ever seen the movie *Holes*? It's about a bunch of kids who partook in a criminal act and had to decide whether to go to jail or to Camp Greene. Little did they know that by choosing to go to the detention camp instead of jail, they would be digging themselves into more than they expected, quite literally. As soon as the kids arrived at this camp, they were immediately handed a shovel and had to start digging. They would dig, dig, and dig all day and all night. The warden forced them to dig under the pretense that it would "build and shape their character," but in all reality, the warden wanted them to find this hidden, lost treasure that had been kept away for over 100 years.

Don't we sometimes feel like that as Christians when it comes to reading our Bible? That we are just digging and digging to no end, and reading the Bible can be a detention camp? I know that when I was younger and even in my teen years, I couldn't stand to read my Bible. I was always told, "Michael, you need to read your Bible. It might get you saved."

I hate reading in general. It's something that I have always tried to avoid; my teachers literally had to force me to sit down and use the entire class period to read and then tell them what I had learned from that chapter. So, when it came to reading my Bible, I thought it was a punishment. I used to think I was reading for nothing and just digging an endless, meaningless hole. I mean, the Bible was just an old book from many, many lifetimes ago.

Can I tell you something? I had never been so wrong in my life. It was the very fact that I did not know the Word of God that I missed the importance of it. I would read it but treat it just as I did when my parents yelled at me. In one ear and out the other, but in this case, in both eyes and out my brain. Have you ever felt that way?

I hear people all the time say, "Well, I don't need to read my Bible. I have a personal relationship with Jesus, and I have experienced firsthand all of these miraculous encounters." Well, Praise God for that! Having encounters with God is absolutely amazing, it really is! I love and strive to have personal encounters with God on a daily basis. But a relationship can only go so deep if there is no personal communication between the two.

You might be tempted to say, "But Michael, come on now. Like, for real? You said so yourself that you can't stand to read. In fact, you said that you hate it! Do I really have to read the Bible to have a relationship and know Jesus?" Yes, I did say that. Yes, I did feel that way. But I love to get to know the Father more intimately and deeply than I do the things I dislike. So yes, you must!

We must realize that studying the Bible and breaking down each individual verse opens up something so supernatural that it cannot be explained with human words. "In the beginning was the Word, and the Word was with God, and the Word was God" (John 1:1 KJV) "and "the Word became flesh and dwelt among us, and we beheld His Glory, the Glory as of the only begotten of the Father, full of Grace and Truth" (John 1:14 KJV).

Kenneth E. Hagin once stated, "The written Word reveals to us the Living Word." I love that. As the verses above says, God is the Word, and the Word is God; and Jesus came down, and the Word became flesh. So, in truth, when we study the Word of God, we are actually having one-on-one time with the Holy Trinity. How so, you may ask. God is the Word, and the Word is God. Jesus came making the Word flesh, and when Jesus was crucified, He entered in us and made our bodies His temple. Making God's Word come alive inside of us, and the Holy Spirit bringing forth the revelation and interpretation of Scripture.

I firmly believe that when we sit down to study and meditate on the Word of God, we are sitting in a small corner of Heaven with the Father, Son, and Holy Spirit. Isn't that awesome to think about? It doesn't just bring some goose bump tingling feeling but brings us to an intentional encounter with God through His living Word! I love how Smith Wigglesworth puts it: "I can't understand God by feeling. I can't understand the Lord Jesus Christ by feelings. I can only understand God the Father and Jesus Christ by what the Word says about them. God is everything the Word says He is. We need to get acquainted with Him through the Word."

That says it all for me! As I said, encounters with God at the altar and in worship are absolutely amazing! Hearing amazing teachings and messages from your pastor is very much needed in growing, but you need to open your Bible for yourself and listen to what the Lord is trying to speak to you.

I absolutely love what Pastor Darryl Baker said in an article he wrote: "You cannot live in the Word only by listening to what a minister of the Word teaches. Jesus, remember, is the Word that became flesh and dwelt among us. We also know the Word of God is Truth. If you spend time abiding in the Word with a focus on getting to know Him, you will know Him, for He is the Truth, and He (the Truth) will help set you free from the things of the life trying to take you captive. One of the number one things that causes this is lies and deception. If we don't know the written Word, we won't know the true Living Word, and we will fall for lies about Him that are not true."

It is so true! We must spend more time than just attending a church service and hearing what the preacher tells us. We must open our own Bible and store His words in our own hearts, not just our ears and brains. There are so many scriptures throughout the entire Bible that tell us to do so. From the front of the Bible to the end, it speaks on the importance of the Word of God and what it really does for us.

> "For the word of God is living and active, sharper than any two-edged sword, piercing to the division of soul and of spirit, of joints and of marrow, and discerning the thoughts and intentions of the heart." Hebrews 4:12 ESV

Here are a few more passages that highlight the importance of staying in the Word: 2 Timothy 3:16, Romans 15:4, Psalm 119:105, Mark 13:31, 2 Timothy 2:15, Psalm 119:11, Psalm 119:18, Psalm 119:130, Proverbs 30:5, Joshua 1:8, Job 23:12, and John 20:31.

I cannot stress enough the significance of what it truly means to dig into God's Word, to study and meditate on these scriptures that He has laid out for us to thrive on! One of the Hebrew words for meditation is 'See-akh,' which means communicating, musing, babbling, deeply considering, pondering, studying, and putting forth thoughts. 'See-akh' is the English translation of the Hebrew verb for mediation. That means to put into action. As you see, the definitions for 'See-akh' that stand out most are studying and communicating.

When we meditate on the Word of God, we not only read and keep it in our hearts, but we have one-on-one communication with God. We enter into a moment of communion with the Father. Communion is not just something we do once every so often; it also means having a close relationship with someone (according to the dictionary). When we think of communion, we think of the last supper, with bread and wine. What if i told you that Jesus in the Bread of Life? "Jesus answered, 'It is written: Man shall not live on bread alone, but on every word that comes from the mouth of God'" (Matthew 4:4 NIV).

"The teaching of your Word gives light, so even the simple can understand" (Psalm 119:130 NLT). When we open up our Bible, we open the doorway of the everlasting light, the light that has created everything and anything in it. It allows that very intimate moment of communion with the Father to come in through His Word and pierce through anything standing in the way of Jesus (the Bread of Life) coming in and fulfilling you with the essentials you need to be sustained.

It is essential that we keep ourselves in meditation and reverence of God's Word. God's Word is our backbone, and He says to be ready at all times. We want to change the world and lead a movement of God so badly, but we don't put in the effort to study His Word and use it to the potential that God has put there for. It is time that we Christians stop leaning on our own understanding and start leaning on God's Word and His promise!

While I was reading a book by Dietrich Bonhoeffer, and as I read these words of his, "I am interested in whether the church, as the church and individual Christians as a Christian, can make a real difference, a redemptive difference."

Studying this and meditating, I felt the Lord speak to me. "The church has a duty as the church to preach the Word of God and the fullness of it, and each individual Christian has a specific duty that God has called them to do. Will the church rise up and be the body of Christ? Will the individual Christian rise up and be the vessel? Our bodies need the blood vessels to transport blood, oxygen, nutrients, and all these things to the entire body so that it can function. We are the Blood of Christ! Rise up!"

How can we be the vessels that God needs to carry out the specific duty He has called us to do if we don't know His Word?

"The revelation of Jesus Christ, which God gave him to show to his servants the things that must soon take place. He made it known by sending his angel to his servant John, who bore witness to the Word of God and to the Testimony of Jesus Christ, even to all that he saw. Blessed is the one who reads aloud the Words of this prophecy, and blessed are those who hear, and who keep what is written in it, for the time is near" (Revelation 1:1-4 ESV).

It is time that we become God-chasers. It is time that we dust off the front cover of our Bible and open it up. We must dig deeper into our calling by going deeper into the very thing that sustains us: the Word of God.

I want to give you ten ways to help you study and dig deeper into God's Word, which can lead you to that deeper, more intimate relationship you have been searching for with God.

1. Plan time for regular study/meditation.

• Set aside 30-45 minutes daily, or however long you want to go. Study for hours if you can!

2. Keep an open mind. Be willing to admit you were wrong and change.

3. Pray for understanding.

• Before you open your Bible, pray that God will enable the words to speak directly to you and open your spiritual ears to hear the Holy Spirit.

4. Let the Bible speak.

• It is our job to study and meditate on the Word but also to be still and listen for the voice of God to speak to us. Don't run your brain a thousand different ways trying to figure out and understand. We will never be able to fully understand God. Let the Spirit speak and interpret for you. He speaks directly from the Father and what the Father wants you to hear. You can read the same verse a hundred times and get different revelations every time!

5. Seek instruction and correction.

• The Bible is a living guideline to instruct us on what we need to be instructed on and what needs to be corrected. Seek His correction humbly; it's what a good Father does.

6. Study different topics.

• Go deeper than what is in plain sight; study what the topics are. For example, if I want to study Scripture on God's peace, I will use a concordance or surf the internet to find cross references and other similar topics to get a broader understanding.

7. Use a study aid.

• There is nothing wrong with using a study aid; use what you can to go deeper into the Word of God. A study Bible is a great tool to have in your pocket!

8. Compare different translations.

• I like to use at least three different translations when meditating on verses. I use my King James Version, New Living Translation, and The Message. Sometimes, I like to use the 1599 Geneva Bible on a Bible app on my phone.

9. Take lots of notes and do word studies.

• Write down everything that pops out at you.

• The Lord will give you revelation while you read; always write those down!

• Do word studies on words you might not be 100% sure of.

10) Obey God's Word and prove it right.

• Put what you learn and read into action. We read not just to know the Word but to take in the light that it sheds so we can take it and illuminate a dark world.

I challenge you today—and I know this might be different than what you are used to—to take this and use it. I challenge you to open your Bible more and study more than you ever have. To read and break down the Scripture verse by verse. It is time that we take hold of the severity of keeping God's Word in our hearts and obeying His commands. It is time that we, as Christians, individually and as the church, study and know the Word of God.

It is time to get rid of dull Christianity and open the Word that is sharper than any double-edged sword and be prepared! We are living in the days where we need to know what we are talking about. We must prepare the way for the Lord! So, in conclusion of this, I urge you to start taking 30 minutes a day and get lost in the Word of God. Shut everything and everyone away for a little while and immerse yourself in His words. Study it and meditate on it. See what God will begin to do in you and your family's life.

Pray with me,

"Lord, thank you for loving us so much that you sent your Son Jesus to earth and become your Word wrapped in flesh. We get to live with your Word living in us and through us daily by letting Jesus in. It amazes me that your Word is living and breathing today as it was two thousand years ago. Lord, I want to be saturated by your Word and your presence. After reading this, I understand more and deeper the importance of keeping your Word and teachings close to my heart, for they are the lifeline to which I breathe you in. Lead me and teach me to go fur-

ther into my relationship with you by spending time with you. I want to learn your words and hide them in my heart as you teach us to. I want to be transformed by the renewing of my mind by fixing it on you, Father. Let it penetrate and resonate with my spirit and speak to me. Lead me to discipline myself to make the time for you. Whether or not life gets busy, I want to seek you most of all. Be my first priority, and set my heart on you. I thank you for all the wonderful things you are doing both in me and around me at this very moment. I thank you for all these things and declare them in Jesus' mighty name. Amen."

Chapter 3
Where is the Love?

"It's easy to talk about how much you love God, but loving others reveals how much you truly do." -Elizabeth George

Where is the love? I read that title, and my mind automatically starts singing The Black-Eyed Peas song, *Where is the Love?* Thankfully, you don't have to hear that; my wife is the singer in our house. Well, that is, until I am in the car alone with no one to judge my flat pitch and failed attempts to harmonize with the radio. In all seriousness, I do have to ask a very important question to all who will hear: Where is the love of God that we Christians should be showing?

I have seen and been guilty of not showing the love of Christ. It might be towards a neighbor who doesn't keep the grass cut against the HOA's wishes. Or the homeless person asking for food. How many times have I just walked on by without even batting an eye? In today's world, it is hard to tell if it is just a scam or hoax, but even then, shouldn't we at least try to represent Christ? You are right to be cautious. However, there are many ways to show the love of Christ other than giving money.

We could offer to pray with them, invite them into a store to pay for food or a beverage, and share Christ along the way. It reminds me of Peter and John in Acts (ch. 3), healing the crippled man. A man who was born unable to walk would be carried to the temple gates called Beautiful, and every day, he would beg all those who were entering the temple. I'm sure there were people filled with compassion for him and gave to this man so he could eat and drink.

When Peter and John came to the gates, the man begged them for money. Peter said, "Silver or gold I do not have, but what I do have I give you. In the name of Jesus Christ of Nazareth, walk". Peter pulled him up, and the cripple was immediately healed. Now, I am not saying to start going up to people asking for money and start yanking them up in Jesus' name. I know the intentions are great, but the outcomes may not be as glorious as the man outside the gate called Beautiful. There very well could be a situation that would call for that, but please use wisdom and discernment from God first.

I used that specific example for this reason: Peter could have just walked right past the crippled man, as many people probably were as well. But

Peter was so filled with the love of Jesus that he reached out to this man in a way that silver and gold never could, to his soul.

He was able to see this miracle manifest because of the power and authority he had within him due to the blood that was shed, the stripes that were taken, and the body that was broken on the cross. Jesus Christ showed His love for us when He died on the cross and rose again on the third day. That same power lived within Peter, giving him the authority to speak boldly and the faith to back it up. It was because of this love that the man was healed and given a gift more precious than gold.

One of our essential jobs as Christians is to show the love of Jesus. I love this quote I read from Mother Teresa: "Each time anyone comes in contact with us, they must become different and better people because of having met us. We must radiate God's love." That is such a powerful statement. Our love for God must radiate into how we treat other people.

I have worked in the food service industry for most of my adult life, serving tables, management, etc. Can I tell you about one of the most hated shifts for most servers? Sunday lunch right after church. I always worked nights, but I heard all the stories about the Christians who would come in all high and mighty and treat the servers and staff like they were trash. I have been told so many stories from several different servers about how terrible these shifts can be. My heart broke every time I heard those stories. I'd assumed Sunday morning serving shifts couldn't be all that bad. The servers were exaggerating, right?

Well, not long after, I was tight on money and needed the extra cash one week, so I picked up a Sunday morning shift. I'm a good Christian guy, so I went to work thinking it wouldn't be that bad of a day. I was wrong. A few weeks later, I picked up another Sunday morning shift. Though it wasn't the worst experience—because I would talk to people about church and ask what the sermon was—I could still understand why my coworkers were hurt and frustrated.

I witnessed on several occasions where a server would walk off crying and angry at God that His people would treat them like that. I had a conversation with one of them, and she said, "I used to believe in God, but it's the people like them that pushed me away and kept me away." I will be honest with you, I was infuriated. I wanted to walk up to that table like Jesus did at the temple and start flipping tables over. I would hear people tell their servers, and even me, "I only have to give God ten percent; why should I give you more?" If I didn't need that job, I would've told them exactly why.

I've heard someone say once before, "Oh, you don't want to give ten percent? That's fine; it's the Old Testament anyway. The New Testament says to give everything!" That is me trying to be funny;

I promise it's better if you tell it in person. All jokes aside, I now see why the after-church crowd can be such a dreaded time. All the church pamphlets, alongside minimal tips and rude behaviors, can push people away from God. If that is how we are attempting to show the love of God, then love! I am not against leaving pamphlets with the tip, but give twenty percent or more if you can.

I have a stack of pamphlets and the million-dollar question (are you saved?) bills in my closet from the ones thrown on the ground or in the trash. Most of those are because I have witnessed other servers get them with a ten percent tip or less, and they scoff while tossing the pamphlet in the trash. Other times, I have witnessed a nice note written in it with a great tip, and the server smiled and kept it. When love and compassion are shown with genuine authenticity, it has more of a profound impact on those we are trying to reach. We must learn to love people according to the Word, or there is no power behind it.

> "Life's most persistent and urgent question is, 'What are you doing for others?'" -Martin Luther King, Jr.

In Greek, there are four different words for love. One of them is Eros, a romantic love. Secondly is Phileo, a friendly kind of love. Thirdly is Storge, a familial love. Lastly, there is Agape, a self-sacrificial love. There are different ways that we can love people. The love that I have for my wife is different than the love I have for my brother or a friend.

The Bible teaches us different ways to love. It teaches how to love our wives as Christ loved the church. A familial love like 1 Peter 3:8 tells us, "Finally, all of you should be of one mind. Sympathize with each other. Love each other as brothers and sisters. Be tenderhearted and keep a humble attitude." NLT. An Agape love like John 15:13 tells us, "Greater love has no one than this: to lay down one's life for one's friends." NIV. This is the love that Jesus has for us, and it is the greatest example of love He taught us. After the last supper, Jesus washed His disciples' feet, knowing that Judas would betray Him.

During those moments, Jesus gave us a very simple yet sometimes hard commandment: "So now I am giving you a new commandment: Love each other. Just as I have loved you, you should love each other. Your love for one another will prove to the world that you are my disciples" (John 13:34-35 NLT). This Agape love transcends all others, the one Jesus gave us. Though it may be the hardest type of love to offer, it is the greatest.

If we are unwilling to show others a sacrificial kind of love, how can we show the love of God? Yes, the other types of love are important and have their significant roles, but Jesus has commanded us to love as He has loved. He showed us all four types, but the Cross was the greatest love He ever showed us.

The Bible tells us not to be selfish and to look out for just ourselves; it says to think of others more than ourselves and look after others more than we do for ourselves (Philippians 2:3-4). To be able to do that, we must love each other with a sacrificial love. The way that we treat others is a direct commandment from Jesus. I know that can be a challenging task to complete, but we must try.

What are some ways that we can make changes in how we show our love in a Christlike way? We can learn to become slow to anger. We can learn to put others' needs above our own. We can learn to be better doers of the Word than just hearers. We can volunteer with local outreaches or ministries to help those in need. Seeing and partaking in something like that can change our perspective on how we treat others. If you have children at an appropriate age, I encourage taking them on an outreach.

How about outwardly showing more compassion to those who are in need? We can walk by someone or know someone who is going through something and feel sympathetic on the inside but not do anything to show it outwardly.

Sometimes, saying "I'm sorry" and "I'm praying for you" doesn't help. Showing actions of love can leave or create a more significant impact than solely using words. I'm all for using kind words and talking with someone about their situation. Words are powerful; the Bible teaches us that the power of life and death is in the tongue. We can speak life into people with our words, and we can also speak death to each other if we are not careful. But actions should back up our words.

I am a firm believer that actions can speak louder than words, and how we walk speaks louder than how we talk. We can say all the right things to people, but if we turn around and our actions are speaking the opposite, where is the authenticity in it? How can someone trust that the words we just spoke over them were genuine if we aren't living up to what we are saying? I like to call it genuine authenticity when how we communicate and walk are in stride with one another. That's how we should be as Christians.

How do we live out genuine authenticity? Well, we start by developing and growing a godly compassion for others. Having compassion goes hand in hand with loving others. The Merriam-Webster dictionary defines compassion as "sympathetic consciousness of another's distress together with a desire to alleviate it." The word compassion can be traced back to the Latin origin of *Compati*, which means "to suffer with."

When we reach out to show compassion towards others and do so in godly love, we actively demonstrate God's grace and mercy. If someone has fallen and we lower ourselves to be with them in that time of need, we are showing them that they are not alone and we will suffer with them to get them back up. That is the Gospel in itself. God so loved the world that He sent His only begotten Son (John 3:16). Jesus was sent to suffer for us so we could be saved. God's compassion for His children is the cross.

Life can be difficult for us all at times, and we might not always feel like being loving and compassionate to everyone. I know that I don't feel like that all the time. We are all human and fall short of the glory of God. We are not perfect people; there has only been a single perfect One, and that's all that will ever be.

I don't know about you, but I am still a work in progress. I have always said that God does not call for perfection, but He does call for pursuit. I challenge myself, and I challenge you as well in this. Let us learn to love more like Christ loved us. That has been a prayer that I try to pray over myself as much as I can, "Lord, let me love like you love."

That might seem like an impossible task, but I want it to be something I pursue every day of my life. Colossians 3:12 tells us, "Therefore, as God's chosen people, holy and dearly loved, clothe yourselves with compassion, kindness, humility, gentleness, and patience." NIV. This verse tells us to clothe ourselves with compassion, which means we are to put it on and carry this love within ourselves like the clothes on our backs. We are to wear the robe of humility with sleeves of compassion, the shoes of kindness and gentleness laced with patience. Equipped with these, we can walk in the love that Jesus has called us to everywhere we go.

If we clothe ourselves in these garments and learn to walk in this love, then the love of God will radiate from within us and shine brightly into this world for all to see. The love that Peter was walking in when he reached his hand out to a lame man, whom countless people scoffed at, was a love so strong and authoritative that it brought healing and peace.

> "Praise be to the God and Father of our Lord Jesus Christ, the Father of compassion and the God of all comfort, who comforts us in all our troubles so that we can comfort those in any trouble with the comfort we ourselves receive from God." -2 Corinthians 1:3-4 NIV

It is our duty as Christians to be so filled with the love of Christ that it directly affects how we love others. How can we say we are filled with Christ's love if we show anger, greed, hostility, and impatience? The world should know us by how we love, but I am afraid we are known for being people who no longer live up to those standards. If we live with anger, greed, malice, and frustration as our common emotions, then we are not living by the leading of the Spirit. The Bible tells us that the evidence of the fruits of the Spirit is love, joy, peace, kindness, etc.

The scriptures also tell us that if we want to live in the Spirit, we must keep in stride with the Spirit (Galatians 5:19-25). This means that if we're going to live a life full of the love of Christ, showing Christlike compassion to others, or the love of God in general, then we must continuously chase after God and walk in the Spirit. The scriptures say it clear as day in those verses: if we want to live with the fruits of the Spirit evident in our lives, we must be in stride with the Spirit.

We must be diligent in keeping the Spirit actively with us step by step, no matter what the pace may be. We must let Jesus in and let the Spirit lead and guide us every single day. I know it is impossible to never let anger, frustration, or any of those feelings in. We are emotional people with many things that pull us from every side. Feelings get high, emotions get stirred up, and lines get blurred. I get it; I really do. I remember times when those emotions were a huge part of my life.

I am reminded of someone I dated off and on for many years in high school and after. We fought, yelled, and got way more jealous than we would like to admit. Anger became one of the most common emotions that I felt. Not because she was a terrible person or anything, but because I was living apart from Jesus. I dated another girl for a few months, and she broke up with me because she said I was always angry and too toxic to be in a relationship with. I was not living in stride with the Spirit. Anger has run deeply in the McAllister family's veins for many generations, and I believe it became a generational curse. However, when I gave my life back to Christ, I noticed that a new pattern began to form. I began to chase after Jesus and fix my gaze on Heaven, and I say with complete confidence that the generational curse was broken.

I can say that confidently because I have been married to my wonderful wife for almost seven years and never yelled at her. Not one single time. She might disagree with that, but it is true. Sure, we have gotten into our fair share of arguments, and tones have been elevated, but nothing like the arguments that went down before Christ became the centerpiece of my life.

I was once screaming at the top of my lungs, veins bulging, and trees became my punching bag where I would pour out my anger and jealousy. Now the fruits of the Spirit are evident, and that is what I want to chase all the days of my life. We must make Jesus the centerpiece and give Him our lives. Not just our hearts but our lives.

When we do this, we can begin to love more like Christ and show the compassion that can only come from Heaven. Being in stride with the Spirit is the direct gateway from the love of Heaven flowing through us into others. We must change the narrative and the questions that the ones who do not believe are asking. Instead of them asking, "Aren't you a Christian? Where's the love at?" Let's get to the point that forces them to ask questions like, "Why are you so nice all the time?" or "Why do you care so much?" Then, we can tell them about the love of God that has forever changed our lives and plant the seed in their hearts.

Remember, it is our job to plant the seed or bring water to the seed that is already planted, but it is God's job to make it grow (1 Corinthians 3:6-9 NLT). We are the ones to sow the seeds of faith into others, and love is the greatest seed we can sow (1 Corinthians 13:13 NKJV).

Pray with me,

"Heavenly Father, I thank you for your deep love and compassion for us. The Agape love that you have shown us. I can never fully understand it, but I am so thankful for it and give you all the praise you deserve. God, I ask you right now to speak to my heart and breathe your love into it. Breathe your compassion for others into it. If there is any malice in my heart or any other fruits of the flesh that are showing more than the fruits of your Spirit, purge me of it right now in Jesus' mighty name. By the power and authority of Jesus Christ, I declare and command that all

fruits of my flesh be gone right now. Only the fruits of the Spirit are welcome, and devil you have no authority. My Father's Word tells me that by Jesus, through the Cross, I step in authority to crush the serpent's head. And I crush the head of these serpents trying to keep me in my flesh right now, in Jesus' Name. Teach me, Lord, to love as you love. To love others, your children, deeper and more Christlike than I have before. Your love is the greatest seed that I can sow into another; I desire to sow into your harvest. Forgive me for not loving others as you have commanded me to. I know that there will be days that I will fall short, but teach me how to give and live in your grace on those days. Empty my heart of all that I have stored in it and begin to fill it with your life and the evidence of your Spirit and its fruits of being in stride. I love you; I thank you, and give this all to you in Jesus' name. Amen."

Chapter 4
We are Unbroken

"Before God could bring me to this place He has broken me a thousand times." – Smith Wigglesworth

Have you ever heard someone talking about being broken before God? Or have you ever been broken before God yourself? If you have, or even if you haven't and this is new to you, have you asked what it really means?

Being broken before the Lord means that we are so grieved in the spirit and stirred that we become rattled before the throne. The power of God shakes us down to the core in such a way that we enter such a holy and agonizing pain. A pain for the lost, a pain for the hurt, a pain for the lonely, a pain for knowing sin.

We have become so comfortable in this modern Christianity that we are not broken before God. We are not so stirred in our spirit to where we have deep emotional pain. There is no agony, there is no godly sorrow. We are so unstirred in our Spirit that it has almost become abnormal to be broken before the Lord. Who is laboring in prayer for the broken? Who is weeping over the children and the lost? Who is praying, "God break me, let me feel the pain of the lost and broken? Bend me, o Lord!" Sadly, you don't hear this anymore from the pulpit and prayer circles.

We live in a day where brokenness is high, but not in the right way. We feel broken beyond repair but don't want to fix it because it is what it is. Society says you are depressed and mentally broken, so they give you medicine to cover it up. I am not knocking down mental health or trying to belittle the sufferings of many, but let me tell you something: God can mend any brokenness. However, I find that people don't want help from others, especially from God. Our self-God complex says we don't need a higher power or anyone to make us feel complete.

We have turned to "put it out in the universe, and the universe will give it back if it is right." I also hear "manifest it," like we have the power and authority out of our own selves to manifest something in the universe. Why wish upon a star when I can bring it to the one who created them? I see a people living with an "I can do it myself" mentality. I don't see many bringing their brokenness to God, laying it all on the altar, and waiting until God breaks it or binds it. We, as Christians, must become broken before God again.

Do you remember the song *The More I Seek You*? If not then take a second to look the lyrics up. I interpreted the lyrics as becoming broken and bent before the Lord. His love is so overwhelming that we can't stand. It is time that we enter so boldly into the throne room that we immediately fall onto our knees in the presence of our Savior.

David Wilkerson was a mighty man of God, and I love to listen to his sermons and the power of God they bring. One sermon in particular I listen to once a month, at the very least. Pastor David brings a call to anguish. It is so powerful and brings me to tears every time I listen to it. He says this:

> "Whatever happened to anguish in the house of God? Whatever happened to anguish in the ministry? It's a word you don't hear in this pampered age. You don't hear it. Anguish means extreme pain and distress. The emotions so stirred that it becomes painful, acute, deeply felt inner pain because of conditions about you, in you, or around you. Anguish, deep pain, deep sorrow, and agony of God's heart. We've held on to our religious rhetoric and our revival talk, but we've become so passive, our so-called awakenings are stirrings

> that last but a short time. And when the short-lived reviving's and awakenings comes, from the hand of God, they are so short-lived, and in those times, we promise God we'll never return to our passivity. But it's not long; it's just weeks or months, and we're back, and this time, we slip further back into passivity than when we started. I speak from experience. And we say this time, God, you've touched me for life, and I'll never be the same. And it's like fireworks, a loud bang and a lot of noise, and then it dies."

How many times in church meetings or conferences has this been me? How many times has it been you? How many times is it that I have been so moved by the Spirit that I wept and wailed before God, but left the meeting and returned to my everyday life. I was broken before God, but only for a short time. As Pastor David said, it was like fireworks—there were a lot of sparks and bursts of glory popping, but it was so short-lived that it only lasted hours or a few short days.

I do not want to live and walk in my faith like that. I want to live every day of my life on this earth so strong in the Spirit that demons are jumping out of windows when I walk into a room. I want to be like the shadow of Peter, so full of Jesus and His power and authority that just catching the shadow of Peter brought healing to people. How can I expect to have this power and authority of Jesus bursting out of me if I cannot be broken and bent before the Lord?

I stumbled upon this quote from Vance Havner that moved me so powerfully. He said, "God uses broken things. It takes broken soil to produce a crop, broken clouds to give rain, broken grain to give bread, broken bread to give strength. It is the broken alabaster box that gives forth perfume. It is Peter, weeping bitterly, who returns to greater power than ever." This moves me so powerfully. When we are trying to go through life on our own terms and power, there is no fertile ground. There might be a crack in the surface here and there that a seed can fall into, but why have a few sprouts from dry ground when we could have a full harvest?

King David paints a beautiful picture of agony and brokenness for God in Psalm 51. For context, this takes place after David committed adultery with Bathsheba and had her husband killed to try and cover it up. David brings God his guilt and sorrow for committing such a sin. He pleads with God to have mercy on him, to wash him clean from this guilt, and purify him.

In verses seven through eight in the NLT, David says, "Purify me from my sins, and I will be clean; wash me, and I will be whiter than snow. Oh, give me back my joy again; you have broken me, now let me rejoice." He then says in verse seventeen, "The sacrifice you desire is a broken spirit. You will not reject a broken and repentant heart, O God." I love the way the Amplified version puts it: "My [only] sacrifice [acceptable] to God is a broken spirit; A broken and contrite heart [broken with sorrow for sin, thoroughly penitent], such, O God, You will not despise. "King David knew the only way for his guilt and shame to be lifted was to come before God, broken and bent.

While in my ministry internship, I learned much about chasing brokenness before God from my spiritual father, Pat Schatzline. We had many conversations and prayers that would sound like this: "Break me, O Lord, let me feel what the lost feel. Let me feel what those who hurt feel, Lord, let me feel what you feel for them. Bend us, God." There were several times when Pat would get on the stage and pray and plead to God before the congregation, "Bend us, Lord." When we pursued in prayer and worship for God to bend us, His Glory would always break out.

What exactly are we saying when we ask God to bend us? According to the Merriam-Webster Dictionary, some of the definitions to bend as a verb are these: *to force back to an original straight or even condition, to guide or turn toward, to adapt to one's purpose, to make submissive.* When we are coming before God, asking Him to bend us, we are asking Him to rain His presence down so heavily on us that we are forced back into the position and purpose of our original submission towards Him. We are acknowledging that there is no other choice but to become broken before Him so that His love and presence can enter in and mend us back into who He has created us to be.

Back in 1904, a great welch revival broke out. A young Evan Roberts and other students walked to the early morning service and sang the entire way there. The song they sang was "It is coming, it is coming, the power of the Holy Ghost; I receive it, I receive it, the power of the Holy Ghost." As the service was ending to break for breakfast, Seth Joshua ended his message with, "Oh, Lord. Bend us!"

Evan Roberts was so deeply stirred by this that it became his very prayer for the revival. "That is what you stand in need of,' said the Spirit to me. And Oh! In going through the door, I prayed within myself, 'Oh! Lord, bend us." Roberts proceeded to the next meeting, where he recounted the meeting and said, "I fell on my knees with my arms on the seat before me, the perspiration poured down my face, and my tears streamed quickly - until I thought that the blood came out.....I cried, 'Bend me, bend me, bend me; Oh! Oh! Oh! Oh! Oh!'"

Evan Roberts was brought before God and, as Pastor David Wilkerson said, baptized in the waters of anguish and became broken before God. Roberts prayed and sought God to bend him until he felt he was sweating blood. That can only be done by extreme anguish and pain. Roberts became one of the key faces and leaders of the revival, which lasted for several months and accounted for almost 100,000 salvations. This reminds me of Jesus praying in Gethsemane before His betrayal that would lead to His death.

> "He prayed more fervently, and he was in such agony of Spirit that his sweat fell to the ground like great drops of blood." -Luke 22:44 NLT

In Matthew 26:38, Jesus said to His disciples that He was crushed with grief to the point of death. Jesus was so broken before the Lord that his physical body was at a point where he felt death. He was crushed under the weight and agony of what He knew He must do. Jesus was praying in the garden in such agony and grief that Luke tells us that Jesus began to sweat blood.

Can you imagine being in such agony and brokenness, praying so fervently that you begin to sweat blood? How could this even be possible, to sweat blood? There is a condition called Hematidrosis, or Hematohidrosis, which is a very rare condition that causes you to sweat blood from your skin even though there are no wounds. What triggers Hematidrosis is not exactly known because it is so rare. It is thought that it could be related to your body's "fight or flight" response. It is also believed that it can be caused by extreme distress or fear, such as facing death, torture, or severe abuse.

Jesus was in deep anguish because He knew what was coming and soon. He prayed that God would take this cup from Him; He was broken for what was to come and in such extreme stress and fear. Some may read that and think it impossible; Jesus was not scared of anything. Yes, Jesus is—and was—the Son of God, but He was just as human as you and me.

If He was not frightened, then why did He sweat blood? Jesus knew He was facing torture and certain death. He was bathing in the waters of anguish, but He knew what must be done. I can only imagine how broken He must have felt in that garden. However, in that brokenness and agony, Jesus came out of the garden in peace and obedience after time in prayer.

Because of this, Jesus sacrificed himself on the cross so that we can find refuge in Him. Because of this, we can have a relationship with our Heavenly Father and come to Him for anything. Jesus was perhaps the most agonized and broken one of us all. Who else could have done what He did? No one.

With this great sacrifice, I feel that our duty as Christians is to be broken before the Lord. I believe this because God so loved the world—you and me—that He sent His only son to be nailed to a cross for our salvation.

A love like that needs to be shown to those who don't know or haven't experienced it. We can only become the true vessels who release this kind of love if we are broken and bent. We must pray for God to baptize us in the waters of anguished so that we can feel the burden of the lost and know what we are fighting for every moment of our lives.

We must become broken for the lost, broken for the hurt and lonely, broken for the ones in need, broken for the Glory of God! We are the clay, and God is our potter; we must come to the end of ourselves, with all the breaks and cracks, and surrender to Him. Just as David brought his broken spirit before God so that He could mend David back into the man he called him to be so we must do the same.

Pray this out loud and boldly.

"Heavenly Father, bend us. Bend me so that I can feel what you feel. Bend me to feel the burden of the lost and hurting. Jesus, I want to be broken in you so that you can mend and shape me into exactly who you have called me to be. Take me to the waters of anguish; baptize me in it and in your fire. Holy Spirit, come upon me so heavily that I cannot stand in your presence. Lord, I don't want to try to hold it together myself. I need you to take over. Teach me, lead me. Let me behold you so that I can carry you

everywhere I go. Let it not be a short-lived feeling but an outwardly lived expression. I submit it to you. Take it all, Lord, so I can give it all for your glory. Thank you for your sacrifice and for enduring what you did so that I could be where I am today. It is all because of you, Jesus. In your mighty name I pray, amen."

CHAPTER 5
Life Without Repentance

"True repentance involves a change of heart and not just a change of behavior." ~ Ezra Taft Benson

Throughout my life and Christian walk, I have always heard the word repent. I think it's safe to say that most—if not all—of us have a general understanding of what it means. Repent for your sins and ask for God's forgiveness. Easy enough, right? At least, that is what I have always thought. If I messed up and asked God to forgive me, I have repented and am made new. Can that really be all there is to repentance, though?

I remember growing up in Sunday school and hearing a fellow student say, "Well, I have already asked Jesus into my heart, and now I'm saved. So, I will live how I want to live, and later, when I'm older, I'll repent and ask for forgiveness." I was certainly no theologian at the ripe age of nine or ten, but I remember thinking to myself, "That can't be right."

Modern theology says that once I ask Jesus into my heart, then that's it. No need to live a life of repentance or turn away from bad habits or sinful patterns. I have spent a lot of my time as a Christian caught in that same mindset. For the longest time, I believed I could say things like, "I'm sorry, God, I messed up; please forgive me." Once I said that, I repented and went on my merry way, doing the same things all over again. I remember times in my life when this was a dark cycle I put myself into.

I would go out to parties or throw them myself, live exactly how I wanted to in unbiblical ways, and ask for forgiveness later. My mindset was that I could go out and drink, do drugs, have sex, and party in any way I desired. As long as I prayed before going to sleep, telling God I was sorry and asking for His forgiveness, then I was good!

Can I tell you something? That is not what repentance is—not even close! I had no clue that what I was doing was prostituting the grace of God. All I knew was to say sorry, but I always wondered what it meant to repent. Is it something super spiritual, a prayer, or an apology to God? Let's jump into a deeper study and find out what it really means!

More than an Apology

As we just learned, in my walk with Christ, I caught myself in a loophole of apologizing to God daily. In my studies, I have found that repentance is not an apology but something totally different.

In its original language and translation, the word apology does not even mean to say, "I'm sorry". To my surprise, it was a defensive word! Our word apology comes from the Latin word *apologia*, rooted in the Greek words *Apo- and logia*, derived from *logos,* meaning "speech." These words together can be translated into "speech in defense." This is also where we get the term apologetics from for defending our faith. I love how the Merriam-Webster Dictionary defines it:

> "The modern apology generally involves an admission of wrongdoing and an expression of regret for past actions, while an apologia typically focuses on explaining, justifying, or making clear the grounds for some course of action, belief, or position."

When I was living my sin-centered life, I was not repenting to God each night like I thought I was. I was talking to God in a defensive manner, admitting that I had remorse and felt bad for what I had done, but that was it. I was apologizing in a self-justifying way, knowing that I would continue down the same path that I was on, the same course of action. No behavior change—or heart change—would follow my repentance. I knew what I was doing was wrong, but I did not want to stop the pleasures I indulged in. I lived this way for many years before genuinely repenting.

When we say that we are sorry, we are acknowledging that we are in the wrong, but we usually will choose to continue the path we are already on. On that path, I always found that I would feel more remorse, sorrow, and pain rather than feelings of peace, grace, and love. True repentance does not bring those feelings of shame but of the other.

> "True repentance never leads to despair. It leads home. It leads to grace."
> -John Ortberg

What does it mean to repent? It means to change one's mind, which can be translated as "to turn around" from the Hebrew word *sheenbeyt*. That is the standard agreed-upon meaning of repenting. In my study for this, I have come across a deeper meaning for it. The word *sheenbeyt* comes from two root words: *sheen* and *beyt*. The root word *sheen* means to consume or destroy, and *beyt* refers to a house or a tent.

The finding in this study led to the literal meaning of *sheenbeyt* in Hebrew, meaning to destroy or burn the house down. So, according to this, when we repent, we are to destroy the house of sin that we have built ourselves in, burn it down, and never return. I was blown away when I read this. It is more than turning around or changing one's mind. It is a complete flip, a making of new real estate. Immediately after I read that translation, I felt the Holy Spirit speak and put this into my heart.

"We have made God the blueprint, but not the finished construction. We have made the foundation in the shape of Him *but without the concrete. We have made* Him *the shingles but not the roof. He is the siding but not the beams. This house has been made on shifting sands rather than on His solid foundations.*

The rains may come, and there may be no leaks. However, how quickly will a house built on a weak foundation fall when the storms come? If our house, our spiritual foundations, are not built right, our house will fall. This true repentance is saying to take these houses that we have built and burn them to the ground. God may be the shingles keeping the rain out, but our walls are built with sin, and they will surely rot and give way with time.

When we truly repent, we must destroy the houses built with the mud of sin and let God rebuild them with the bricks of Heaven. We must turn our ways and change our hearts to face the Heavens. We are prostituting the grace of God by asking for forgiveness with our apologies instead of our repentance. If we are not turning away from the sins we ask God to forgive us for, then we are just habitual apologizers, never living in the trueness of repentance. Saying I'm sorry to God when we sin but not turning away from it is saying we love that moment of self-pleasure in our flesh more than our relationship with the Father."

When I was the furthest away from God, living in more sin than I ever had been; I still came to God every night, if I wasn't too drunk or high to forget, asking God to forgive me, saying that I repented for my sins. Honestly, the only reason I did that was because I was scared that if I died in my sleep, I wouldn't go to Heaven. I never truly repented, though, until I reached my lowest point.

I was standing on top of a water tower, thinking about jumping off. I remember looking down questioning if my life really mattered and what would happen if I just jumped off. I remember it so vividly, but I also remember what came after those thoughts. I heard a whisper in the wind "I have more for you than this." I knew immediately that it was the voice of God. That was the moment that led to my true repentance.

The morning I walked into a rehab facility was the morning that I burned down the house of sin that I was living in, and God began to build a new one in me. That old house I used to live in is just a pile of ash I have never looked back at.

> "Repent, then, and turn to God, so that your sins may be wiped out, that times of refreshing may come from the Lord." Acts 3:19 NIV

I am afraid if we do not turn away and choose not to burn down the house of sin we have built within ourselves, we will miss the great things our Father wants to give us. God wants all of us, not just parts of us here and there when He feels like it. Our Heavenly Father wants to shower us with blessings and things beyond our thoughts. How can He give us these things if we aren't giving ourselves to Him entirely? We can buy, make, and be given things from friends and family that can make us happy. But it is the things given to us by God that matter the most.

We can only find salvation and eternity in Heaven in one way: through our belief and faith in Jesus. We can only be given this incredible gift by repenting and accepting Jesus as the Son of God who hung on the cross to die for our sins. It is only through repentance that we find life in Christ.

Jesus told His disciples in Matthew 16:24-26, "If any of you wants to be my follower, you must give up your own way, take up your cross, and follow me. If you try to hang on to your life, you will lose it. But if you give up your life for my sake, you will save it. And what do you benefit if you gain the whole world but lose your own soul? Is anything worth more than your soul?" NLT.

I think Jesus is painting a wonderful picture of repentance here. To be His disciple, we must cast everything else away. They must turn away from everything they have ever known and not hang onto their past, or they will lose what is in store.

Jesus asked the disciples if there was anything in their lives that was worth losing their soul for. There is no going back to what you once were. I know this sounds like a tough thing to do, and it very well will be for most of us. We all fall short of the glory of God; we are an imperfect people constantly at war with the flesh. Want to hear something great, though? God still loves you and calls us to come back home when we fall short.

I have said this so many times and will say it more times to come. I believe that God does not call for perfection but pursuit. There was only one—and will forever be only one—that was perfect: Jesus.

I love the story of the prodigal son because I can relate to it so much. The son asked for his inheritance from his father and left his home after receiving it. He went to a city full of ungodly things and indulged himself in all those things. Just as I did. He was living a lavishing life that many people could only dream of. He probably had nice clothing, the hottest new camel, and an expensive tablet.

I can imagine that he would throw some of the biggest parties on the block, and everyone wanted to be around him. However, he soon ran out of money and found himself working in a pig's pit and eating the worst scraps he could find. He was ashamed of what he had become and for wasting what his father had given him. I think that he knew he could go home anytime, but he thought his father would be ashamed of him and reject him.

How many times have I felt like that? I remember a time when I looked in the mirror and was disgusted with the person staring back at me. I think that the prodigal son felt the same as I did. But one day, the son decided that enough was enough, gathered what he had left, and began his journey back home. He knew that his father would be angry and disappointed with him when he returned, but working as a servant for his father would be better than where he was at that time. He recited and rehearsed what he would say when he met his father, wondering how bad it would be.

What he didn't know, though, is that his father sat in the fields every day looking to the horizon, waiting for the day of his son's return. Even though the son took his inheritance from his father and left him in the dust, the father never stopped loving his son. I can imagine the father in the field watching, waiting, praying, until he caught a glimpse of his son returning. Maybe the son saw a glimpse of his father, too, but was still full of shame and guilt. Still reciting his excuses and rehearsing the words he was to say.

This is such a beautiful parable because this is the love of God! When the father saw that his son was still off in the distance, he didn't wait for him to come to the gate. The father ran to his son and immediately met him with an embrace of love. He threw his robe over him, and the father put his ring on his son's finger and loved him so deeply. The son thought that he would be met with anger or disappointment, but it was the exact opposite.

It doesn't matter how far we may fall or walk away. God's love is always there, waiting and watching for His sons and daughters to return to Him. God will meet you exactly where you are, no matter what you have done or said, and meet you with love. The son built a life, a house of sin. He knew he could go home but was too ashamed to, but just like me standing on that water tower, enough was enough. I was ashamed of who I had become, but I had to turn away from that because I knew my Father still loved me.

So, I did what the son did in the parable: I turned from where I was living, let it burn to ashes, and never looked back. God brings beauty from ashes and wants us all to be made beautiful in Him. God is never mad at you, but madly in love with you.

Let's pray,

"Heavenly Father, I thank you for your love. Thank you for the love that brings beauty from ashes. Teach me to repent and pick up my cross to follow you daily. Teach me to not look back at my past but to look forward to my future and purpose in you. Thank you, Jesus, for your sacrifice on the cross so that I can repent and be your disciple and find eternal life. Lord, I know I will still fall short at times, but teach me to get up and keep going. Even if I fall back into sinful patterns, you still have new mercies for me every day. I know I can still find my life in you by giving mine for your glory. Let me be made new in you and your image. Lord, teach my heart and mind to repent and turn my face towards you. Make me new. I love you, Father, and I thank you for who you are. Teach me to chase you every day and build a new house with the bricks from Heaven, and let your Spirit be the mortar to hold it together. Thank you, Father. In Jesus' mighty name, I declare and solidify this in the courts of Heaven. Amen!"

Chapter 6
Religion Over Righteousness

"Consider then, O man! whether there can be anything more wretched and poor, more naked and miserable, than man when he dies, if he be not clothed with Christ's righteousness, and enriched in his God." -Johann Arndt

Have you ever heard someone use the phrase that being a Christian is not about religion but about a relationship? I remember hearing that for the first time and was shocked by the thought. We are taught that Christianity is a religion, which in its contextual purposes it is. It is the world's largest religion, with an estimated 31% of the global population, according to a baseline study in 2010 by Pew Research Center. That is roughly 2.3 billion people and is estimated to grow to around 3.3 billion by 2050. That is an incredible number to think about! However, I must wonder how many of those 2.3 billion people who declare to be Christian have an active relationship with Jesus.

There are so many people that I have met who proclaim to be Christians, but there's no evidence of an active and lively relationship with Jesus. Is it that we are born into a Christian family and jump on board choosing it to be our religion? Or maybe we have an encounter with Jesus asking Him to come into our hearts, only to continue to our lives the same as we always have?

Let's recap my testimony to paint a fuller picture of the time I was backsliding and living apart from my relationship with Jesus. I grew up believing that I was a Christian because I would attend Sunday school and evening services. I went to church and proclaimed I was a Christian but without a personal relationship with God.

It wasn't until I was thirteen that I had a personal encounter with Jesus and gave my life to Him. For the next several years, I lived on fire for Jesus and was baptized in water and in the Holy Spirit. I felt the call of God on my life and knew exactly what God's purpose for me was.

Fast forward a few years, and I began to fall away from God. I walked away from my daily relationship with Jesus and pushed Him to the side. I still proclaimed to be a believer while becoming quite the partier. I found myself many times drunk at a party, trying to preach to people and tell them about Jesus. Without even realizing it, I very quickly became just another religious person.

I read once someone describing being religious as someone who outwardly practices, but their heart and soul are not in it. I would openly talk about my beliefs and how great God is outwardly, but inwardly, I wanted to live how I wanted to at that moment. My mouth professed, but my heart did not confess.

In my study of the origin and meaning of the word "religious," I found that there was no word for religion in ancient Greek, in which the New Testament was written. The two closest words were *eusebeia*, meaning piety, and *threskeia*, meaning cult. (Before anyone accuses me, no, I am not saying that religions or religious people are cults. There can be separate groups of people who take things way too far and out of context and can become one, but I am not saying that at all.)

While studying the word for religion in Hebrew, I came across a study stating that the modern Hebrew word for religion, *dat*, is a word rarely found in the Old Testament, meaning law, decree, or order. Though there is speculation about the word's true origin, it is ultimately found rooted in the Latin word *religio,* meaning "reverence for God or the gods, careful pondering of divine things, piety, the *res divinae (divine matters)."* Its usage within the Latin language and dialogue closely refers to the performance of ritual obligations.

Going deeper into the study of that word, I found no significant or spiritual meaning to it. I don't want to be the one to burst any bubbles, but I think I might have. When we are referring to being religious in a biblical sense, it is in the sense of following the laws and decrees.

Remember, the Old Testament was originally written in Hebrew, and the loosely translated words used are laws, decrees, and order. The New Testament was originally written in Greek, and there were no words for being religious written in Jesus' time. I write all of this simply to say that Jesus did not call for us to be religious but righteous disciples and follow His commandments.

I see more religious believers leaning towards a legalistic stand, believing that good works and merits will keep them in good standing with God. Thomas R. Schreiner said, "Legalism exists when people attempt to secure righteousness in God's sight by good works. Legalists believe that they can earn or merit God's approval by performing the requirements of the law."

When we study the Bible, even though it does not mention the term legalism, it is taught throughout by the Pharisees. Jesus teaches us about it in Luke 18:9-14: "To some who were confident of their own righteousness and looked down on everyone else, Jesus told this parable: 'Two men went up to the temple to pray, one a Pharisee and the other a tax collector. The Pharisee stood by himself and prayed: 'God, I thank you that I am not like other people-robbers, evildoers, adulterers-or even like this tax collector. I fast twice a week and give a tenth of all I get.' 'But the tax collector stood at a distance. He would not even look up to Heaven, but beat his breast and said, 'God, have mercy on me, a sinner.' 'I tell you that this man, rather than the other, went home justified before God. For all those who exalt themselves will be humbled, and those who humble themselves will be exalted.'" NIV

.

Even though the pharisee was a "religious" man of God, he still lacked a key characteristic Christians should chase after daily: righteousness. Unlike the words *religion* or *religious*, which are not anywhere in the Bible or loosely translated in some versions, the words *righteous* or *righteousness* are mentioned in the Bible hundreds of times.

Some translations use it more than others, some less. According to an article published by Living Word Chapel, the Bible mentions the word *righteousness* 540 times compared to *faith*, which is mentioned 348 times.

Christians should all believe that the Bible is God-inspired, God-breathed, and written by humans through God by His Holy Spirit. So that means that God is telling us to seek His righteousness, and being righteous in His eyes is one of the most important components of our faith. Sadaq, the Hebrew word for righteous, means to be just and righteous in conduct and character. To be just means to be honorable and upright, being truthful, and standing for what is morally right. It is to have godly integrity in all that we do.

I love the testimony of Paul. He was one of the most legalistic people there ever was until he had an encounter with the King. I love what he wrote in his letter to the Philippians 3:5-11. He paints a detailed and beautiful picture of his transformation from religious to righteous.

> "I was circumcised when I was eight days old. I am a pure-blooded citizen of Israel and a member of the tribe of Benjamin—a real Hebrew if there ever was one! I was a member of the Pharisees, who demand the strictest obedience to the Jewish law. I was so zealous that I harshly persecuted the church. And as for righteousness, I obeyed the law without fault. I once thought these things were valuable, but now I consider them worthless because of what Christ has done. Yes, everything else is worthless when compared with the infinite value of knowing Christ Jesus my Lord. For his sake, I have discarded everything else, counting it all as garbage, so that I could gain Christ and become one with him. I no

> longer count on my own righteousness through obeying the law; rather, I become righteous through faith in Christ. For God's way of making us right with himself depends on faith. I want to know Christ and experience the mighty power that raised him from the dead. I want to suffer with him, sharing in his death, so that one way or another I will experience the resurrection from the dead!" NLT

Paul followed the laws and decrees almost perfectly, performing the rituals of the Pharisees as they pertained to their divine matters. But when Paul was met on the road and had an encounter with God, he switched from chasing the religion of the Pharisees—what they said was right—to chasing after what Jesus taught as righteousness before God, and look at the incredible testimony he left for us to read and study in the New Testament.

Paul switched his focus from trying to mirror what the Pharisees and their laws wanted to be preached to focusing on righteousness through Christ and becoming a direct reflection of Heaven. We must chase righteousness over religion.

I am not trying to belittle or shame anyone who is religious and say that you are not truly saved. Please believe me when I say that. I am never one to throw rocks or point fingers at people. I will stand in the fire with you and walk with you through it. In the intro to the book, I mentioned that there is never condemnation, as Romans 8 tells us, but there is Holy Spirit conviction. So, if anyone is feeling fired up at this moment, I would encourage you that this might be a good place to take a pause, kneel, and pray before continuing.

There are so many Bible verses that pertain to being righteous, practicing righteousness, seeking righteousness, etcetera...Being righteous before God is such a crucial part of our daily lives and our journey in faith. If we follow what the Bible says but do not seek righteousness, then why even follow its teachings? Proverbs 21:3 tells us that practicing righteousness is more acceptable to the Lord than sacrifice.

Righteousness is something we can strive for every day, something that we can always increase in and practice our faith in daily. When we live striving for righteousness, the blessings of God will follow—the seek-ye-first-the-kingdom-of-heaven-and-all-else-will-be-added-unto-you kind of blessings.

How can we make a shift and begin to chase the righteousness of the Lord? First, we must acknowledge and accept that righteousness is never in our own merit or doing but fully the Lord's by His grace and mercy. We can never achieve the righteousness of Christ without Christ being the center of it all. To pursue God's righteousness, we must first be made morally upright in His eyes through justification. When we accept Jesus into our lives, we are justified and made right in His eyes. Because of God's love for all His children (John 3:16), Jesus paid the ultimate price for all our sins and made us whole in God's eyes.

However, it is only when we accept Jesus and are saved into the Kingdom of Heaven are our spots made blameless. Even though we are sinners living in a sinful world, the love God has for us is so deep, and He wants to have a relationship so badly with us that through the giving of His son on that cross, we are justified and have the opportunity to make a choice that alters our eternal destination.

> "Consecrate yourselves, therefore, and be holy; for I am the LORD your God. Keep my statutes, and do them; I am the LORD who sanctifies you" (Leviticus 20:7-8). ESV

Sanctification is our journey of chasing after Jesus, our everyday walk of seeking His face. The word sanctify in Hebrew is *qadas (kaw-dash),* meaning to keep oneself sacred, holy, purified, and set apart. After we are justified by faith in Jesus, being sanctified is the everyday choice of keeping what is holy. Paul tells us in Philippians 4:8, "Finally, brethren, whatsoever things are true, whatsoever things are honest, whatsoever things are just, whatsoever things are pure, whatsoever things are lovely, whatsoever things are of good report; if there be any virtue, and if there be any praise, think on these things." KJV.

I believe Paul is giving us an example of how to seek sanctification. As we just learned, the Hebrew word used for "sanctify" means to keep ourselves in the holiness of God and to be pure and set apart.

Have you ever heard of the saying, "One of our biggest enemies is our inner me?" That can be so true, right? Especially in today's age, when every turn we make seems to have something keeping our minds distracted. I know it is for me; I have said before that it's so hard for me to concentrate sometimes because I have "E.A.D.," also known as easily amused disorder.

That's a bad joke, right? I can just hear my wife saying now, "Don't you speak that over yourself; I rebuke that in Jesus' name!" She would be right, though: don't speak those things over yourself. In fact, don't even think those things about yourself.

We can find ourselves getting lost in our thoughts so easily. I can't tell you how many times I have started a thought that had the purest intentions and somehow led to a stream of thoughts that do not match Philippians 4:8 at all. To me, the battle of sanctification starts in the mind. Yes, I say battle because it is always a war in my mind to fix my gaze on Heaven. We are all going through things in the busy, fast-paced, modern world that we live in.

We have careers, families, kids, pets, hobbies, etc.... that pull on the strings of our thought patterns. However, I have some good news for you: though there may be many battles, the war has already been won. When we align ourselves with Heaven and have Jesus in the center, we operate from a position of victory.

When we let Jesus in and let the Holy Spirit take the lead in our hearts and minds, it becomes easier and easier to keep that mindset that Paul modeled. If we keep the mindset of "I am already victorious" when we face things in life, the journey of sanctification can become a pace that we are in stride with. We are called to be separate from the ways of this world as a representation of Jesus. We are called to seek the Kingdom of Heaven and spread the Gospel. We are called to walk in holiness and pureness. By our faith in Jesus and His sacrifice on the cross, we are made right in God's eyes by justification.

Sanctification is dying to ourselves daily and picking up the cross. It is setting ourselves apart from the world and not chasing what the world does. It is chasing after God, becoming disciples of Jesus, being doers of the Word, not just hearers. When we do these things, our lives will be significantly impacted by obeying God's Word. When we do these things, we chase after the righteousness of God.

Pray this prayer after me.

"Heavenly Father, thank you for your love and the sacrifice you made so that we can be made whole in your eyes. Thank you, Father, for casting my sins as far as the east is from the west when I accepted you as my Savior. Lord, teach me how to seek and chase your righteousness. I know that I am made right and justified in your eyes because of the sacrifice Jesus made on that cross. Teach me to seek sanctification in you daily. Your Word tells us that this life is not a sprint but a marathon, so I know that it will be a journey and not an easy one, but speak to me and lead me in it. Teach my heart, Father, to not have a religious spirit but to seek righteousness in you. Keep me away from pride and self-righteousness. A religious spirit led the Pharisees to put you on that cross, denying your majesty; Lord, if a religious spirit in my life hinders me from you, I nail it to the cross right now in Jesus' name and speak your power and authority to take over. I desire righteousness over religion. I want your fullness in my life; I need your fullness in my life. Thank you, Jesus, for what you have done and are doing right now. I am a child of God; I have been called and will answer the call. Lead me and direct me in your ways, always. In Jesus' mighty name! Amen."

Chapter 7
Where is the Unction?

"With all thy getting, get unction, lest barren altars be the badge of our unctionless intellectualism."
-Leonard Ravenhill

Growing up, I never really learned much about the Holy Spirit; in fact, I don't remember any sermons preached in that small-town Alabama church ever mentioning the Holy Spirit. I recall hearing about Jesus, God, and all the Bible stories taught at VBS, but never anything about the power or importance of the Holy Spirit. Within the church's small congregation, there were various thoughts and opinions that if you spoke in tongues, it was not of God but of the enemy.

I do not mention that to shame or discount anything about that church but to show an example of how many of us have lost touch with the power and importance that the Holy Spirit has in our lives. I never knew of the power and authority the Holy

Spirit brings in and through you when you are filled with Him. Looking back, I can recall my first encounter with the Holy Spirit, and I am so thankful for the events that led me to that encounter.

My best friend invited me to go to a summer camp where his dad was preaching in Springville, Alabama. Coming from my church background, this was an entirely new world. This event was in a massive auditorium filled with hundreds of kids. Growing up, my youth group was around fifteen to twenty, and half of them were my cousins.

The youth and Sunday school I was used to was singing from the hymn book to a piano while everyone was in sync with monotone voices. There is nothing wrong with singing hymns to just a piano; it is a beautiful way to worship God and give our praises to him. However, my thirteen-year-old self was about to be forever changed at this summer camp.

I remember sitting there, weirded out at first because I had never seen anyone lift their hands in worship before, and I was surrounded by at least three hundred kids praising God in a way entirely new to me. I was encountering church like I never had before. I was encountering God like I never had before. I was praising God like I never had before. I lifted my hands and sang as loud as I could. It was like a rushing wind blowing into my spirit, and that was the day that I encountered the Spirit of God for the very first time and gave my life to Jesus.

That was the day that I decided to join the family of Christ, and my life would never be the same.

You see, I grew up going to church and learning about the Bible and its stories, but I was learning how to be a surface-level Christian. (Again, please do not take this the wrong way. I want to clarify that I am not expressing any hatred or shame towards any church or the body of Christ. My intention is to emphasize the significance of the Holy Spirit actively operating within us.) The man preaching that night, Pat Schatzline, became my spiritual father. The leading of the Holy Spirit and Pat having the unction to listen and follow that leading has changed and shaped the lives of countless people. I am a living example of that.

After that camp, I was on fire for Jesus. Nate and I would travel with Pat to different camps and conferences during the summer before football camp started. My life was literally turned upside down and still is to this day. Life at home was not the greatest at this point in my life. Things were happening, and it wasn't good to be around, so I spent most of my time with Nate's family. I was at their house so often that I had my own basket in Nate's room to make a cot and a list of chores with my name on it. Being there, I was given the blessing of watching Pat, a man who was chasing after God and being led by the Holy Spirit, which allowed me to learn and deepen my own relationship with God.

We were at Branded by Fire youth camp in Pensacola, FL, the very place where the Brownsville Revival broke out in the 1990's. I remember laying on my face, weeping and crying out to God when I felt a hand on my back. It was like the hand was a foot long, and it was cold, hot, and tingly all at the same time.

Startled by this, I jumped up to see who it was, but no one was around me. I was surrounded by a sea of students on their faces crying out to God, and I heard a voice whisper in my ear, "Look around; this is what I have called you to." That was the first time I heard the voice of God; it was clear as day, and I remember it like it was just yesterday. I was fifteen years old then.

At that same altar the very next year, I was baptized in fire (Matthew 3:11). Ever since that night at that first summer camp when I was thirteen, not only did I choose to follow Jesus, but I chose to let His Spirit take the wheel and lead me. When I let go and let God take over by the leading of His Holy Spirit, my life shifted, turning towards a new direction and a life that I never saw coming. I went from being spiritually dead to spiritually set on fire, and my life can never be the same. I must do all that I can to keep that fire alive and let the Spirit lead. Of course, there are seasons when I am not where I need to be. I have strayed and let the fire dwindle, but I have tasted His goodness too many times to let that fire completely die out.

I look around at many churches and Christians today that are not on fire for God, and I have caught myself asking the same question: Where is the Holy Spirit? Where is the unction in the church and the body of Christ? Where are the churches, the pastors, the leaders, the brothers and sisters in Christ who let go of everything and let the Holy Spirit take control? Where are the altar calls where we meet God face to face to be filled again? Where is the hunger for God? We need unction back in the body of Christ!

I see so many Christians walking around saying that they love God and want to be used by God but are spiritually dead. It seems that we have allowed ourselves to become a candlelight burning within instead of a lantern illuminating the darkness around us. There are churches that proclaim themselves Christian but are publicly allowing evil at their podiums. I can tell you where I think we have slipped to allow this to happen: we have lost the unction.

There's that word again. What in the world is unction? I kept hearing that word repeatedly in my spirit as I spent time with the Lord one evening. I had never heard that word before, so I started to read *Why Revival Tarries* by Leonard Ravenhill, and the very first chapter was on unction. I had to do my homework to find out what this word meant.

According to the King James Bible Dictionary, unction means "the act of anointing" or "that which excites piety and devotion." Having unction means to live and operate in the anointing, being led by the Holy Spirit, and chasing the glory of God with reverence and devotion. It is to live with such a burning desire for God that all else seems to fade away, and your gaze is set on Heaven. Your countenance becomes a direct reflection of Heaven.

Strong's Concordance has it defined by the Greek word χρίσμα (Chrisma), meaning anointing. It refers to the teaching ministry of the Holy Spirit guiding the receptive believer into the fullness of God's perfect will. When we have unction, we have a special anointing from the Holy Spirit to chase after the fullness of God's will in our lives and for those around us. As Christians and the body of Christ, must get back to the place of unction if we want to be who we are called to be in the fullness of Christ.

How do we make a shift and chase after this unction? I love how Leonard Ravenhill said it in his book I mentioned earlier: "Unction cannot be learned, only earned by prayer. Unction is God's knighthood for the soldier-preacher who has wrestled in prayer and gained the victory. Victory is not won in the pulpit by firing intellectual bullets or wisecracks, but in the prayer closet; it is won or lost before the preacher's foot enters the pulpit."

Our Heavenly Father is calling us into knighthood for His Kingdom, to be mighty warriors marching into battle. Just as the Bible tell us to put on the full armor of God because we are in a spiritual war with the forces of darkness. The enemy has fiery arrows, but when we are clothed with the armor of God, they cannot penetrate. When shots are fired at us, we have a shield of faith to raise up to defend ourselves from any weapon the enemy may try to use. When our shield of faith has been bombarded by attacks and life hits us from all angles, it may start to put some dents in the shield.

Life hits us all; sometimes, we are hit with hard blows that will crack even the strongest shields. I know that my faith has been hit hard recently, so hard that it left some dents and cracks in my shield. This past year has been one of the hardest years my wife and I have had. We ended 2022 feeling great about 2023 and what was to come. Our daughter was born in 2022.

I was in my first active year in real estate, and I was doing great in it. Things were really starting to look up for us financially, and we were sure that we would be stepping into our full-time ministry calling. We thought that 2023 would be our best year yet, but it has been one of the hardest trials we have faced. I was excited and ready to quit my job serving tables to be a full-time realtor, but overnight I lost all my desire to be a realtor. I let my license sit and did nothing with it while still paying all my monthly fees and dues.

My wife is a stay-at-home mom with our daughter, and serving tables has become our only source of income. I got sick and ended up testing positive for COVID-19 for the first time, and I was out of work for eight days with no pay. As soon as I recovered, my wife got sick, so I had to stay home for several more days to take care of our daughter so she didn't get sick.

I was out of work for a few weeks with no sick pay, and we spiraled downward very quickly into a bad financial situation. I went from being scheduled to work five days a week to only three days. The restaurant was overstaffed and not allowing as many hours per employee. I couldn't pay our bills. I could barely put food on the table.

I immediately started applying for jobs to try and make ends meet, but nothing was working out. I think I submitted almost ninety applications, but we were stuck in a rut we did not want to be in. In the middle of this trial, some light finally came shining through. My wife was pregnant with our second child, and we were so happy and in love with the baby already. That news brought so much joy to us in the middle of this dark season. During this time, our lenders were very understanding of our situation and put our mortgage into forbearance so our missed payments wouldn't go against us. My wife pulled out all her savings from her 401(k) to pay bills and make a few mortgage payments during this forbearance.

I finally got an interview with a job and started right away. Things were starting to look up for us, but it didn't last very long. I had to leave that job because I was spending more money on gas each week than I was making, so I went back to full-time serving tables. My wife and I questioned God and asked Him, "Where are you?" We kept getting hit with blow after blow, but we had faith that He still works all things for our good. We were scared that we would lose the house or have to sell it before it was taken from us. We cried, not knowing why all of this was happening but still trusting God and happy that we had a baby on the way to look forward to.

While having the daily fear of losing the house, tragedy struck. Our baby was not measuring at the correct time frame that it should have been. I had never felt more broken in my life; the fear of losing everything was at my doorstep. I am supposed to be a provider and keep a roof over my family's heads, food in their bellies, and clothes on their backs. I was having a hard time doing these things and felt like a failure as a husband and father.

In the middle of all the fears of losing everything, we found out that we would be losing our baby. We fought for weeks and did everything that we could. We had many nights of prayer and tears, but our baby could not fight any longer. I was broken; my faith was broken.

I wanted so badly to be mad at God and blame Him, but I couldn't. My shield of faith had been weakened, and there were cracks in my armor.

Those big blows cracked my shield, and the fiery darts from the enemy never stopped. But I never dropped my shield in the face of my enemy, and even though I could feel the heat on my face from the fiery arrows in the cracks, I never laid my faith down.

Can I tell you something? When our shields are heavily damaged from battle, they can always be mended and welded back to full strength and even stronger. Our faith is built and made stronger in our place of prayer. We had just hit one of the lowest moments of our lives and could've been hit so much harder and just dropped everything, but we didn't. We had people behind us that covered us in prayer, and we never stopped praying.

In the midst of tragedy and mourning, we prayed for peace, and God showered us beyond belief with His peace that surpasses all understanding. Prayer and intimacy with God can mend any wound and refortify our shields of faith stronger and quicker than anything the enemy can throw our way. It is in the fire that metal is fortified and made new again.

My shield was broken, and I was weak for a time, but I got on my face and cried out to our Heavenly Father, and He answered. We can either let the fire from the enemy weaken our armor, or we can meet God in the secret place of prayer to renew it and make it stronger than ever. Our place of prayer determines the quality of our walk with God and the level of intimacy we have with Him.

The functioning of our unction with the Holy Spirit is birthed out of true intimacy with God.

I love listening to Leonard Ravenhill's sermons; there is such power and anointing in the words that come from him. Through all his sermons and words that I've read from his books, one thing that he has said that has been burned into my mind is this: "No man is greater than his prayer life." He wrote in his book that "preaching affects time; prayer affects eternity." Anyone can preach a message, but without it being birthed from a place of prayer and unction, it is just intellectual words reaching intellectual minds. As Leonard Ravenhill puts it, "A sermon born in the head reaches the head, a sermon born in the heart reaches the heart."

To get back to a place where we are led by the guidance and power of the Holy Spirit, walking in the authority that Jesus told us to walk in, we must start in the prayer room. Not in a corporate place of prayer, even though those times are powerful and needed, but in a place of intimacy with God where we can be in a personal encounter with the King. To get back to our place of unction, we must first get our prayer life back to the secret place with God. A place where we shut ourselves in with God and away from the world.

In 1 John, John is writing to fellow believers in a time when followers of Christ were being persecuted and false teachers were persuading people to abandon their faith in Jesus. In the second chapter, he tells us about the false teachers and people leaving the church. But he mentions in verse twenty that those he is writing to are not like the others who have abandoned their faith. They are not like them because they have an unction from the Holy One who knows all things (KJV). Because they received the Holy Spirit and had unction, they had the ability and knowledge to discern when a false teacher would come or an attack from the enemy, and they would not be fooled. With this authority of Jesus living and operating within them, they were able to face the hardest times, persevering and carrying the faith of Christ through them.

There is power in unction. There is authority in unction. There is fullness of God in the unctioning. We, as the body of Christ, must live with unction if we are ever to see a move of God take the world. There must be unction in our everyday walk, how we live, and how we talk. There must be an unctioning in the church and its pulpits. There must be an unctioning in every person who declares that they are a Christian and follower of Christ; it is only by the power and the anointing that chains are broken and lives are changed forever.

> "Away with this palsied, powerless preaching which is unmoving because it was born in a tomb instead of a womb, and nourished in a fireless, prayerless soul. We may preach and

> perish, but we cannot pray and perish. If God called us to the ministry, then, dear brethren, I contend that we should get unctionized. With all the getting-get unction lest barren altars be the badge of our unctionless intellectualism." -Leonard Ravenhill.

When we are active in our prayer life, spending time in the Word and being led by the Spirit, God can use us in the most magnificent and mysterious ways. Jesus tells us that a helper is coming to us when He ascends to the Father's right hand. The Holy Spirit, if we allow Him, will help us in so many ways in our day-to-day walk. He helps us in our prayer life when we have no words to pray, and all that comes out is moans and groans.

With the Holy Spirit within us, those moans and groans are prayers of anguish, and the Father hears them and knows exactly what we are saying. With the Holy Spirit active in our lives, we can be given words of knowledge for someone. We can pray for people in the spirit, and the Spirit can meet that person on the other side of our city or the world.

I remember when I was working at a thrift store. I was bringing out furniture to the floor, and when I saw this lady, the Holy Spirit struck me with a word. I fought it at first, thinking it was just my mind, but I obeyed and went to her and said, "The Lord hears your prayers; He has not abandoned you; trust in

Him." She immediately broke down into tears. She was battling cancer and was asking God why He wasn't answering her prayers.

Another time, I was praying, and a girl that I went to high school with popped into my mind and I was to tell her that God would take care of her sister. I had not spoken to her in years and did not know that she even had a sister. I obeyed and sent her a message saying what the Spirit told me. She replied that she was shaking and crying because it could only be a message from God. She and her family had been praying for her sister to return home and be free from an abusive relationship that she was in.

The sister left that relationship and moved back home, and I believe God did a mighty work of restoration in her. Not only did the Spirit bring faith and restoration back to her sister, but the Spirit was also able to touch the life of my schoolmate and reveal Himself to her and to me by giving the word of knowledge.

There have been several incidences where the Spirit has spoken to me or shown me images that have been faith-building messages to strangers. I do not say that to boast about supernatural gifts that I have been blessed with, but to simply say that when we have unction and are led by the Spirit of God, we can be used in supernatural ways that we would never believe possible. Remember, I came from a small church that did not preach on the Holy

Spirit and the gifts, yet I chose to follow and be led in such a supernatural way that has touched lives in a way that nothing natural or of my own doing ever could. When we have an unctioning that is operating with the Spirit, God will use us in powerful ways that will touch and change lives for His glory, all while building and sharpening our own faith for greater glory in Jesus.

I will be the first to admit that I need to work daily on everything I'm writing and talking about in this book. Life gets so busy that it becomes hard to make time to chase after God as much as I would like. I will admit that at times in my life, I have fallen short in allowing the Spirit to lead me. I had to work on getting back into the secret place where I could just spend time with God in prayer and meditation. At that time, I made excuses as to why I did not have time. I became a lazy Christian.

I was listening to a sermon by David Wilkerson about the cost of the anointing, and he said something that was so profound to me. He said, "God does not give the anointing to lazy Christians." I was in one of my places of prayer where I heard God the most, and I began to weep. I had made myself too busy for God.

Bills needed to be paid. I needed to get a new job. I needed more shifts at work. I sleep until noon most days. Excuse after excuse of not wanting to sacrifice my time to be with God. I did not want to sacrifice ten hours of sleep for five or six to pray, build my faith, and prepare the way for the Lord to come in and use me.

People! We don't have time to be lazy Christians; there is too much at stake and too much work to do. It will be a hard adjustment leaving the comfortable systems and schedules we have made for ourselves. However, I have come to find that believers called by God cannot stay in a place of comfort. We cannot grow to our full potential in the place of comfort. We begin to grow when we leave our comfort zone. When you are working out in the gym, and you keep the same weight and routine, trying to achieve big gains, you will not see the results you want.

How can we grow when we stay in the same place of comfort in our faith? It takes time and effort and boldness to get out of our comfort zone, but we must do it. I can guarantee that Jesus was not comfortable being nailed to that cross, but He knew what it would take to achieve the biggest gain in the Kingdom of Heaven and save His people.

It is time to let the Holy Spirit take the lead again, not worrying about what others may think of us. It is time that we are set ablaze by the Spirit of God and burn so bright that the darkness has no choice but to disappear. We speak of revivals and awakenings and how badly we want and need them, but unless we chase after the unction of the Holy Spirit, we will not see them.

Pastors, leaders, brothers, sisters, young and old, we must shut ourselves away with Christ and let Him baptize us in the Fire and Spirit so that we may face this dark world and let the fire of God shine so bright that the gates of Hell have no choice but to tremble and take back the evil that it has let loose on the earth. It is time that we turn from the candles of compromise to the oils of anointing that set our lanterns ablaze.

Let us pray for the Holy Spirit to move in us; pray this out loud with me with unction and authority.

"Holy Spirit, I ask you right now to come in and take over. Mend my heart and turn my countenance towards Heaven. Father, forgive me of all my sins and give me a new heart today. Lord, if I have let my armor become weak, meet me in the fire to make it new again. Only you can make beauty from ashes, and I place it all into your hands. Holy Spirit, come baptize me in fire and your Spirit so that I can walk in your fullness. Give me unction! I want to burn for you. Come right now and take control of my mind, heart, and soul. I want to walk in your Spirit and your guidance. Thank you, Father, that your Word says there are new mercies for me every day and leads me to choose to pick up my cross. Even when I don't feel like it, even when times get hard and I don't know what else to do, let me always hold firm to you. Let my body be your lantern, and let your anointing ignite the flame within me to burn bright for you. Thank

you, Holy Spirit, for your gifts and for your leading. Thank you for unction! Lead me and teach me to keep it all the days of my life and to share it everywhere I go. In Jesus' mighty name, amen!"

CHAPTER 8
An Unguarded Heart

"In the human heart, there is a built-in obsolescence factor. It does not matter how powerful and influential you are, how much education you have, how self-controlled or holy you consider yourself - your heart, if you do not guard it, will break down." -K.P. Yohannan

Have you ever been like me and been distracted when you should have been focused? Have you ever been in the middle of worship at church or a conference, and while singing, you are thinking about things that you should not have been? I know that I have been guilty of this many times over, especially when I was still young in my faith. I would sing about the mighty name of Jesus and how it changes everything, but in the back of my mind, I was picturing images that I should not have been.

I love what Pastor David Wilkerson said in his sermon, "A Call to Anguish": "We've become like the children of Israel who said the right words, but here's what God said: I've heard the words of this people. They have well said all that they have spoken. Oh, that there was such a heart in them that they would fear me and keep my commandments always that it might be well with them and with their children forever (Deuteronomy 5:29). You have the right words. You sing the right songs, but your heart is not right."

How can we be in the middle of praising and worshiping God and, in the back of our minds, thinking of the wrong things? I know that having a wandering mind is normal and will still happen from time to time, but how can we keep those wrong thoughts from popping into our minds when we are supposed to be in a holy moment with our Savior? We can start by guarding our hearts from the unholy things of this world.

In today's world, being able to guard your heart is becoming more and more of a challenge. It is hard to filter everything completely. The world's morals are becoming seemingly more slippery each week, and keeping evil and negative things out of our conscience is getting harder. It is everywhere we go. Things we may not be able to control and put a godly filter on just slip right on by in obvious and subliminal ways.

You can go into a restaurant and are exposed to very secular music that you do not want to listen to. TV commercials are feeding our eyes subliminal evil messages all the time. I can recall a commercial right now that is so nonchalant about a specific product but is covered with subliminal satanic images throughout the entire airtime.

Some of our favorite cartoon channels for our children are full of them, and they have no clue! These companies do a great job of making it subtle so that it is hard to catch. As we progress even further into corporate wickedness, they are making it more and more obvious because no one is stopping them. I actually do believe that it is even applauded now.

As Christians, we need to guard our hearts and minds more than ever. If we are not careful and keep a very close eye on what we allow to enter our hearts, more of the world and its lustful desires will creep in without us realizing it until it's a serious problem.

Proverbs 4:23 (NLT) says, "Guard your heart above all else, for it determines the course of your life." I love how the King James Version puts it: "Keep thy heart with all diligence; for out of it are the issues of life." What we let into our hearts has a direct effect on the outcome of our lives, present and future.

Luke 6:45 (KJV) says, "A good man out of the good treasure of his heart bringeth forth that which is good; and an evil man out of the evil treasure of his heart bringeth forth that which is evil: for of the abundance of the heart his mouth speaketh." When we guard our hearts and let good, clean, godly in and always try to focus on all these things, our hearts are saturated with good, and good will come out. However, if we do the opposite and let filthy, evil, worldly things in, bad things come out.

> "The seed that fell on the footpath represents those who hear the message about the Kingdom and don't understand it. Then the evil one comes and snatches away the seed that was planted in their hearts." Matthew 13:19 NLT

We have let the world plant seeds in our hearts. Seeds of doubt, seeds of lust, seeds of hate, seeds of self. With all these seeds growing like weeds in our hearts, we have limited the space for the seeds of Jesus and the Kingdom of Heaven to take root. I see so many young people taking to the idea of not needing Jesus or anything to do with God because the world has become so perverted toward the Gospel. The enemy knows what he is doing, using the media and social media to plant seeds that we don't see. We have let our hearts become infertile ground for Heaven's sake but fertile in growth for the kingdom of evil.

Matthew 15:19 says, "For from the heart come evil thoughts, murder, adultery, all sexual immorality, theft, lying, and slander." NLT. Music and entertainment everywhere promote all these things. Even shows for children drop subliminal messages for evil. Enough is enough! We must fight for our minds, fight for the conditions of our hearts, and fight for the minds of our children!

If you have read this far into this book, then you probably see a pattern. I love to use science and facts to prove scriptures. Science and history were always my two favorite subjects, and I just love how science fuels the flame of proof of God and the Bible. Before we jump into all the scientific facts, I must break some more things down for us to get an even better understanding of the power and impacts that lay ahead.

The Hebrew word for heart is "lev" or "Levav." The Hebrews and writers of the Bible referred to the heart as the mind, the conscious, your command center where all your thoughts, feelings, and emotions come from. The ancient Hebrews didn't understand brain function, so they said with all your heart. With all your emotional being, that is what I believe they are referring to. Now, let's jump into some scientific facts!

Studies from a scientific view collaborate with these scriptures on the importance of governing what we accept our eyes to see and ears to hear. *Psychology Today* published an article titled "What Happens if You Don't Watch What You Watch?" to discuss findings about "what goes in, must come out." As I read this article, I was just amazed at how much these statements testify to what the Bible has taught for thousands of years. Check these out.

> "It turns out that what you watch, read, listen to, and play can affect your mood, temper, and even how generous and kind you are to others afterward!"

> "People who watch as little as 15 minutes of 'negative TV news' have shown increases in a depressed mood, anxiety, and tendency to be more 'catastrophic' about their personal worries."

> "Watching violent sequences in movies and TV can lead to increases in blood pressure, heart rate, and galvanic skin responses - and to 'short-term' increases in aggressive outbursts in adults. That is, adults are more likely

> to lose their temper or express anger in a way that is exaggerated soon after watching a violent TV or movie scene (the findings for children are more long term)."

> "On the other hand, watching TV shows and video clips with pro-social themes (like people helping others, problem-solving, cooperating, and being generous) can lead to more cooperation, more positive attitudes, less aggression, and more altruism (behaviors that do not directly benefit the giver, like 'sharing,' 'comforting,' 'donating' and 'offering help')."

Those are some incredible facts, aren't they? I mean, can you imagine how much better and different life would be all the time if we just kept filling and fueling our minds and spirits with good things? Like the Word of God and prayer, your life will be changed forever!

Just like what we are letting in with our eyes and its outstanding effects on our psyche and everyday lives, what we let in through our ears has just as an impact on our spiritual and mental well-being. Are you ready for more scientific facts? Awesome,

I'm glad you said so. John Hopkins Medicine constructed the same kind of study of how music can affect our brains. Remember that our brains, consciousness, and mind are what the writers of the Bible are referring our hearts to. Here are some of their findings and the power of what we let in has on our hearts.

> "There are few things that stimulate the brain the way music does. If you want to keep your brain engaged throughout the aging process, listening to or playing music is a great tool. It provides a total brain workout. Research has shown that listening to music can reduce anxiety, blood pressure, and pain as well as improve sleep quality, mood, mental alertness, and memory."

> "If you want to firm up your body, head to the gym. If you want to exercise your brain, listen to music."

An article written and published by *Graham Psychology* had this finding in the same study.

> "Research findings have demonstrated that music supports our physical, mental, and emotional health. It can help in regulating our emotions, improving our mood, and enhancing productivity and concentration, and it can even help us sleep better."

Those are just incredible findings. Did you know that what you watch and listen to also has this much power in your mind? As these findings have shown us, music and television have a very powerful impact on the health and well-being of our minds and lives. If we are not guarding our hearts with what we are letting in, you can see how it can be detrimental to us. It can cause us to lash out with emotions and reactions that aren't really us.

Before I gave my life back to Christ (I call them the BC days), I was not guarding anything coming in. I would listen to profane music and watch profane things, and I can reflect and see how that impacted how I acted. It directly affected how I talked and even got into things I should not have gotten into.

In my senior year in high school, we would have a fight night before the football games. On the way to the fights, we would blare some specific songs to pump us up and get in the mindset to bring violence. Playing those types of songs had a direct and immediate effect on our minds and emotions as we were on the way. I think back to those days and thank God that I do not live like that anymore.

So, we can see how the wrong kinds of music, movies, and TV can have a harmful and destructive impact on our lives. What if we did the opposite? What if we choose to listen and watch only good and godly things? I am not saying to never go to the movies or listen to secular music. I love going to the movies, and I have a playlist of secular songs that I still listen to. But I must filter and choose the right things to listen to and watch.

I am not listening to those fight night songs while going to the grocery store. I don't need to be ready to throw down with someone over those tomatoes or milk jugs. However, since I gave my life back to Christ, I have more of a desire to listen to praise and worship instead of anything else. I want to be saturated with God's love everywhere I go. That way, if Mrs. Betty is trying to fight me over a tomato to make soup for Sunday lunch, I can hand it over with a smile on my face.

We must fight to guard our hearts. Matthew 13:15 says, "For the hearts of these people are hardened, and their ears cannot hear, and they have closed their eyes—so their eyes cannot see, and their ears cannot hear, and their hearts cannot understand, and they cannot turn to me and let me heal them." (NLT).

If we are not cautious, we can become so saturated with ungodly things that our hearts become hardened. I know that it may be almost impossible to keep everything out, but we must try every single day. Just as the Bible tells us to pick up our cross daily, we must choose daily to be conscious about what we are letting in. We must stand firm and not give in to it.

A compromise here and there may seem like it isn't hurting anything, but eventually, it will become a ditch that is hard to get out of. Matthew 6:21 tells us, "For where your treasure is, there your heart will be also." (NIV). If we do not treasure holiness with God, then our hearts can never live there coinciding. If we are choosing to treasure and keep ungodly things in our lives, even though they may not be the "biggest" issues, our hearts will still be aligned with that instead of the fullness of God.

What we let in determines the quality of our lives and those around us. What do I mean by that? As we have learned from the studies, the things we let in can directly correlate with how we act. It can influence how we begin to talk to people and treat them. If we are just watching and listening to filth and negative things, eventually, we will start to act in some of those ways. An unguarded heart can lead us to have an unfiltered and untamed tongue.

James 3:3-5 says, "We can make a large horse go wherever we want by means of a small bit in its mouth. A small rudder makes a huge ship turn wherever the pilot chooses to go, even though the winds are strong. In the same way, the tongue is a small thing that makes grand speeches. But a tiny spark can set a great forest on fire." It goes on to say, "And among all the parts of the body, the tongue is a flame of fire. It is a whole world of wickedness, corrupting your entire body. It can set your whole life on fire, for it is set on fire by hell itself" (James 3:6 NLT).

The tongue may be impossible to tame; we all say things we do not mean and are sinful. But I believe that when we are filling and fueling our minds, hearts, and spirits with good and godly things, it will be easier to control our tongue. If we choose to put on praise and worship or Christian hip-hop instead of secular music, it can make a positive shift. An inward decision can lead to an outward transformation.

> "Then you will experience God's peace, which exceeds anything we can understand. His peace will guard your hearts and minds as you live in Christ Jesus. And now, dear brothers and sisters, one final thing. Fix your thoughts on what is true, and honorable, and right, and pure, and lovely, and admirable. Think about things that are excellent and worthy of praise. Keep putting into practice all you learned and received from me—everything you heard from me and saw me doing.

> Then the God of peace will be with you."-Philippians 4:7-9 NLT

If we choose to only let in the good and the godly things as much as we can and really begin to saturate our hearts with the peace and love of God, our lives will shift in such a positive way. I believe that we can begin to feel a shift in our minds, spirits, and psyche very quickly if we implement these changes in our behaviors. They might not be an overnight fix, but they will begin to make a change before you know it. I challenge you to start becoming more aware of what is going on around you. Try to notice the little things in what you are watching and listening to, especially in secular music. Satan was the worship leader in Heaven before he was struck down.

The enemy knows exactly what to play and say to catch your ears and mind to keep you away from God. Have you noticed all the satanism that is in mainstream music and its singers? They are posing as demons and devils themselves. The devil is in the details in mainstream music, and it's very evident. I challenge you to begin to listen and watch better, cleaner, and godlier things and see how your heart will begin to change.

I can say that with confidence because I have seen firsthand what it has done to my own heart. I don't talk the way I used to or allow myself to use explicit language. I don't have the desire to listen to or watch things that I have before. The way I talk to people and interact with them is different than what it used to be in my BC days. My heart's desires are more fixed and engaged towards the good things of God and His ways. One of my favorite prayers is this: "Father, let the desires of my heart become the desires of yours." I didn't catch myself praying that while I was listening to songs about violence. But I am choosing to go to war in the Spirit with how I guard my heart and to not let the things of this evil world in as much as I can. I challenge you to do the same.

Go into battle for your mind; remember that guarding our hearts is ultimately guarding our minds, spirit, and consciousness. Whatever is in the heart overflows into your life. Leaving our minds and spirits unguarded allows us to fall into patterns that eventually become habits.

When I was growing up, I would mostly listen to country or alternative music, but when I was surrounded by friends who only listened to rap, I slowly began to change. When I was around them, that was what we all listened to, and when I was alone, I would still play the other genres of music. However, as time passed, I would start to play rap music more and more when I was alone until, eventually, it was all that I listened to. When we are watching the wrong things or listening to the wrong things, we will eventually begin to adapt to the words, lyrics, or actions of what we are saturating our brain with.

Our minds become rewired by what we are allowing in. This process is known as neuroplasticity. It is when the brain rewires or reorganizes itself to create new neural pathways and connections in our brain. Dr. Caroline Leaf, a renowned and revered neuroscientist, concluded that "*the mind governs the brain and determines its functions, not the other way around; the brain is what the mind does.*" She and other neuroscientists have agreed with this conclusion, and their findings are rewriting what we know about the brain and how it functions.

These neural pathways can even restructure our brain and its physical shape. It blows my mind just thinking about that. Our minds are so powerful. That is why it is so important to go to battle over them!

What we are letting in is effective in the way we think and speak, which directly affects on our brain functions and even the physical health of our command center! It is a scary thought that what we allow ourselves and even our children to watch can either build or degrade our brains by having significant impacts on our minds and our hearts, as the writers of the Bible would say. However, there is always beauty from ashes when we let God step in and take control.

Romans 12:2 tells us to be transformed by the renewal of our minds. Just as we can let the negative come in and dig new neural pathways into our brains, we can let the Word of God in and rewrite our minds into new code. I love this so much; how could Paul understand neuroplasticity and its effects when he was writing this. It was and is fully God that he came to that conclusion.

So how do we begin this process of renewing our minds? Dr. Caroline Leaf puts it this way: *"If you're patient and committed, you can completely change your thinking systems by replacing them with new thoughts."* It starts with deciding to begin guarding your heart and making better choices. I have found that in my life, when I listen to worship more, I give praise more, and I have better and healthier thoughts. You can't have a negative mind with a thankful heart. When I watch cleaner things on TV and movies, I have a cleaner mind and cleaner thoughts.

Watching and listening to things that are negative and evil trigger the negative pathways that are trying to build, but filtering out the negative and only letting the positive in overrides those negative pathways and literally rewrites over them! That is so incredible to think about. We can override these negative traits and pathways by fixing our gaze on Heaven. When we want to watch something that we do not need to be watching, put something else on that is godly. When we want to listen to something that can negatively impact us, turn on worship music and begin to praise God.

When I was in rehab, we were still allowed to have nicotine, and it was so hard to break. I was in for a few weeks and kept trying and trying, but I could never get past the third day. I was praying to God, and He dropped into my spirit, "Go read my Word." When I would start desiring a cigarette, instead of just trying to resist, I would go into my room or the library and open my Bible. I didn't know it then, but God was teaching me how to renew and override this bad habit with His power and the renewal of my mind.

I would tell myself I was strong enough and could do it, but I was no match. Only when I let go and fixed my gaze on God did the change I needed and prayed for come. I put my guard up with the Word of God. I put on the full armor of God and guarded my heart by the filter of the Holy Spirit. Only then was I able to make it past the third day. Now it has been over nine years without any desire or temptation to reintroduce nicotine or alcohol into my life again.

"But seek first the kingdom of God and his righteousness, and all these things will be added to you." Matthew 6:33 ESV. Do not leave your heart unguarded to the attack of the enemy. He is like a lion, waiting to pounce on its prey. When we have heavenly guards on our side and the filtering of the Holy Spirit, the enemy can no longer lay claim to any footholds over us.

I want to pray for you, and I want you to pray this out loud as if you are stomping on the devil's head. Say it loud and proud, declaring it over yourself!

"Heavenly Father, I come to you right now with thanks and praise that you have defeated the grave and given me the authority in your name to trample over the serpents. I come to you in that authority and power and declare over myself that I will not be led by the powers of this world and its evil desires. I am standing, declaring, and choosing to guard my heart from these things so that I may live in your fullness. Lord Jesus, forgive me for letting things into my heart that have no business or place being there. I command these strongholds to loosen and be gone in Jesus' name. I am choosing in this very moment to no longer let these things have any power over me because I am free by the power of Jesus, who lives in me. Thank you for this freedom and the softening of my heart. Father, give me discernment as I go through my days to see the things that I have not seen before that are trying to creep their way in. Open my eyes to see the things that you desire for me to see; open my ears to hear the things you are speaking to me. Let the desires of my heart become the desires of yours. Teach me to guard my heart to only let the things of Heaven in so that I may walk and speak in your ways and in your love. Thank you for all these things

as I receive them in the mighty name of Jesus! Amen."

Chapter 9
Relevance Over Reverance

> Only when we are captured by an overwhelming sense of awe and reverence in the presence of God, will we begin to worship God in spirit and in truth.
> – Alistair Begg

Have we gotten to a point where we are more worried about what we are doing is being talked about more than what God is doing? Have we become more concerned about the pulpit, the stage, and followers on social media and what they say we are doing "for the kingdom" more than what God is accomplishing? If we are more concerned about the number of followers or likes someone has on social media, then we are building our own kingdom over the Kingdom of Heaven. What we do only becomes relevant to the Kingdom of Heaven if it is the name of Jesus being lifted high and remembered, not ours.

I have been guilty of wanting to seek the pulpit and my name be known too many times. I remember when I would say that I didn't care about becoming known, famous, or a popular preacher that everyone had heard of. I told myself so many times that I did not care about those things, but I was lying through my teeth because, in the back of my mind, I wanted all those things. I am also guilty of seeking relevance over reverence.

I am not saying that it is wrong to be a famous preacher, singer, or anything of the sort. The bigger the platform, the bigger the reach God has through you. But that is the point that I am trying to make. Are we trying to make the reach through our own doing, or is Jesus on center stage and we are the stagehand? If we seek the stage for our own benefit, then we are hindering the full reach of God through us. If we are center stage and making Jesus our stagehand, then our reach can only go as far as our voice carries.

God will still use you for His anointing on stage; however, if we are the stagehand, the voice of God will go further than we ever could and make an everlasting change. In fact, we, as humans ourselves, cannot make an impact of everlasting change. Only Jesus can, by doing it through us; only the Holy Spirit can speak the voice of God through us. And only God can bring the rain to water the seeds that our obedience to Him plants in others. Without God as the centerpiece and letting the Holy Spirit take the lead, we are but empty vessels trying to be the hands and feet of Jesus without Him.

I am reminded of the verses in Matthew chapter 7 when Jesus tells us that many will come to Him saying, "Did we not prophesy in your name and cast out demons in your name and perform many miracles in your name?", Jesus replies, "Depart from me, for I never knew you.". That is the most terrifying verse in the Bible to me. We can perform miracles and cast out demons in the name of Jesus but never know Him. The name of Jesus carries all authority over the heavens and the earth.

Remember when Jesus and the disciples reached the shore, and the man filled with legions of demons came running down and fell at the feet of Jesus, bowing before Him? I am convinced that the name of Jesus is all that is needed to perform miracles and cast out demons. This says to me that we can do and say all the right things, keeping Jesus as a stagehand. We can have the center stage and speak the name of Jesus, and it will carry the power and anointing to those ready to receive it. All the while, we can preach and lead His people and never fully know Him because we have made the pulpit about us.

How many times have we seen pastors and leaders fall because of their pride? It may start out with Jesus at center stage, but can it be that when we catch a glimpse of the light shining on us we push

Him to the side? Saying things like, "Look what I just did! Look at what I have accomplished! I built this ministry from nothing, and look how great it is!" Has our shining light of relevance covered up or pushed aside our reverence of the One who made all this possible?

There is a difference between taking pride in something you are doing and being prideful. If we keep our eyes on the pulpit more than we are on God, I am afraid that a prideful seed is planted into our hearts. Having people cheering you on and clapping to what you say can definitely begin to let a seed of pride take root if we are not careful. I believe that if I had taken to the pulpit even just up to a few years ago, I would have had a good chance of that happening to me.

Growing up and not coming from much has made me want to make a name for myself and a legacy behind it. A strong and positive name that my children and their children can be proud of. In my family, we take great pride in our last name and the weight that it holds. I believe that my intentions would've been pure, but I'm afraid pride would have snuck through somehow. Now, I can say with confidence that my spirit and soul have become more concerned about the name of Jesus being known more than mine ever will. The name of Jesus is the only name that will carry the same weight behind now and forever, and that is the weight of the world that He took on His shoulders. We can and could never bear the weight that Jesus took on, so why would we want to try and take it in any form?

People are not changed or touched by my words; my words are full of the flesh and its desires. It is the Word of God that speaks through us that brings change; it is the Word of God speaking through us that brings healing. It is the power and authority of Jesus that flows through us and casts out demons and performs miracles. Who are we to think that our words on our own can bring about any such things? That is why the only relevance that we should be seeking is by making our reverence of God relevant everywhere we go. By having and keeping the fear and awe of God as one of the centerpieces of our lives, we can keep our reverence for God greater than our want for relevance in this world.

> "What we, following the scriptures, call the fear of God, is not terror or dread, [but an awe that holds God in reverence]." -Martin Luther.

I was doing a study on what it means to have the fear of God, and I think that it fits perfectly into the point I am trying to get across. (Fair warning of what is about to come; you are about to get a glimpse of how my brain works and the spiderweb of thoughts that come with it.)

Dictionary.com defines fear as: "A distressing emotion aroused by impending danger, evil, pain, etc. Whether the threat is real or imagined; the feeling or condition of being afraid." And "Reverential awe, especially toward God."

Reverence is defined as "a feeling or attitude of deep respect tinged with awe, the outward manifestation of this feeling. A gesture indicative of deep respect; an obeisance, bow or curtsy."

I had never heard of the word reverence much before until I started studying it. And in my word search of what it meant, I stumbled across another word, obeisance, so I did another search on this word. Obeisance means "a movement of the body expressing deep respect or deferential courtesy, as before a superior, a bow, curtsy, or other similar gesture."

We look at fear as something that terrorizes us. That is how the world has perverted it, and so many of us see it as that. Living in the fear of God should not be something that makes us tremble in fear; it should be something so holy and amazing. As these definitions here proclaim, every time I lift my hands in worship or open up my Bible, in public or private, it is out of fear for the Lord. As Martin Luther has said, "What we, following the scriptures, call the fear of God, is not terror or dread, [but an awe that holds God in reverence]." Being in awe means to have an overwhelming feeling of reverence, admiration, or fear. Even to be in awe of God means to fear God.

1 Samuel 12:14: "Now if you fear and worship the Lord and listen to His voice, and if you do not rebel against the Lord's commands, then both of you and your king will show that you recognize the Lord as your God." NLT. To fear God is to be in awe and keep Him in reverence. This verse tells us that if Saul and Samuel want to be used and exalted in the Lord, they must constantly bow down to God. They must humble themselves and show their love for the Lord.

Let's break that verse down: "Now if you fear." Not to tremble and hide but to bow and respect. Dictionary.com has defined fear as "the outward manifestation of this feeling."

What feeling, you may ask? The feeling of being in awe. What does being in awe mean again? An overwhelming feeling of reverence, admiration, and fear! But that points right back to the beginning! Yes, it does!

To be in fear of God is to be in awe of God, and to be in awe of God is to be in fear of Him! This makes no sense; to be in fear of God is to just be in fear, some might still say. Fear is being in awe, and being in awe is to fear. (I warned you about how my brain thinks when I do these studies. Follow me on this, and trust that it will make sense in just a moment.) Let's look at it this way. It is a never-ending circle because God's Word says that He is the beginning and the end, right?

So, it means that you can't just choose it once and it's with you all the way to the end. No, to keep our reverence for God is to fear the Lord with awe in a constant bowing with the most upright respect, overwhelming feelings of admiration, honor, humility, and obedience while living in the outward manifestations of it, which would be the evidence of the fruits of the Spirit. That was a mouthful to get out and to take in. One way to simplify it would be this: Living in fear of the Lord is not an emotion or common thought. It is a habitation of action and choice to stay in a constant bow with humility to God.

When the definition goes on to say "the outward manifestation of the feeling," I'd like to say "choice" there instead of "feeling." What that means is when you choose to live in the constant state of fear and bowing daily to God with honor and humility, then it will transform the outward appearance you put off, giving you a constant manifestation of His presence.

Let's continue breaking down this passage of Scripture. "And worship the Lord and listen to His voice." If you fear, as we just went deep into, then you are living in a constant manifestation of His glory and choosing to stay there and bowing to God and living in fear of Him. Then, you are living in a constant state of worship to Him. When we are there, the Holy Spirit will begin to speak to you, and you will be able to hear Him more clearly, opening yourself up to more than you ever thought possible.

"And if you do not rebel against the Lord's commands, both you and your king will show that you recognize the Lord as your God." It is a constant battle; we must choose to live in that place of fear and surrender. We must fight to stay constant so that we will not fall into a rebellion or the pride of self-relevancy. Also, by doing that, we show God that we are all in this! When we show God that we are all in, He will reveal so much more to us. If we want God to use us to our full potential, if we want to help expand His Kingdom, we must choose to live in the never-ending choice of fearing the awe of God.

I was riding in the car one day with a good friend of mine, and the Holy Spirit spoke this to me. "My God does not work in conformity and complacency; my God works in desperation and authority. With compassion and inherency." I had never heard of inherency before, so of course, I had to do my word study. Inherency is the state or fact of inhering or being inherent. Inherent is existing in someone or something as a permanent and inseparable element, quality, or attribute.

When we choose to live in that never-ending state of honor and reverence to God, also known as fear, we are choosing to step out of the shackles of conformity of this world and step into the Kingdom of Heaven, and He becomes that inseparable element. When we live in honor and respect towards God, it is then when we fully let Him in to become that final sealing quality that will separate us from everything that keeps us from the potential He has in store for us. Jeremiah 32:39 says, "And I will give them one heart, and one way, that they may fear me forever, for the good of them, and of their children after them." KJV. When I study this, it makes me think that God does not want us to be afraid of Him and run and tremble.

He wants us to live in such humbleness and reverence to Him so that we can be kept in constant awe of His love and wonders. So that He can reach down and take care of our every need, and our children's needs, and their children's children. God is saying He will put His Spirit in you to lead you to that reverence we must keep. Because He wants to bless you, and He wants to take care of you! A good father always takes care of his children.

> "For ye have not received the Spirit of bondage again to fear; but ye have received the Spirit of adoption, whereby we cry, Abba, Father." -Romans 8:15 KJV

Webster's 1828 Dictionary says this: "Slavish *fear* is the effect or consequence of guilt; it is the painful apprehension of merited punishment." The devil perverts what fear really should be and wants us to tremble and hide from God. He wants us to fear God like we would fear standing in front of someone who wants to take our life. That is the furthest from the truth; God wants to be near and dear to you. We do not have to fear the consequences if we have accepted Jesus as our Lord and Savior because He bore all of them for us on the cross. We must not let the enemy have a seat at our table and tell us that it's okay to put Jesus as the stagehand.

I think back to when I wanted the limelight of the stage, and looking back now, I believe it was because I was beginning to lose my devotion to God. I had lost my awe for Him. Is it that when we begin to lose our awe and honor for God we start to seek our own self-relevance over our reverence for the Almighty? We must choose to live in the constant seeking of His face and His fame. I have always wanted the spotlight, but not for all the right reasons.

I know that I am called to preach, and there is nothing wrong with being in the spotlight as long as we are not there to limelight ourselves. We are given and entrusted with the platforms to bring the Word of God so that He can impact the lives of others and bring change to hearts. This has been a valuable lesson to me, and I pray that I will always keep it near and dear to my heart. I pray that it will be for you, too.

Pray with me,

"Lord, if I have placed you as the stagehand and kept myself in centerstage, forgive me. It is all about you and only you. I don't want any other name but yours to be remembered and echoed for eternity. Lord, I come to you asking for your guidance in keeping you in front. I want to live in awe of you every day. I want to have a godly fear of you that keeps me humble and reverent towards you and your kingdom. It is "Let your will be done on earth as it is in heaven," not mine. Holy Spirit, speak to my heart and melt any parts that may have turned to stone, from pride or any selfish desires that have kept me from keeping you as my constant. Keep me from seeking any self-relevance that would hinder my relationship with you. Today, moving forward, I just want your reverence over my relevance in this world. My love for you is the only legacy that I need. Thank you for your love and grace, Father, as your Word tells us that you have new mercies for us every day. In Jesus' name, I pray. Amen."

Chapter 10
Belief without Faith, Faith without Action

> *"Faith is a living and unshakable confidence. A belief in God so assured that a man would die a thousand deaths for its sake."* - Martin Luther

When the Holy Spirit first spoke the title of this chapter to me, I didn't think much of it. Other than, "Oh man, that is going to be a good one." Now that I look at it and concentrate on the statement, I think to myself, "What a complicated statement to process." How can we have belief without faith? Doesn't believing mean having faith? People say they believe in their faith, but what is their faith? Faith in Jesus? Okay, but what is your faith? Faith is not your religion. I stand firm on my faith in Jesus.

What is the meaning of faith in this modern day? Let's start with what the Bible's definition of faith was when it was recorded in the Bible in its original text. According to scholars, faith, in the KJV is used twice in the Old Testament and 245 times in the New Testament. The word believe is used 19 times in the Old Testament and 124 times in the New Testament. The numbers are also about the same in other translations, such as NASB, NIV, and NRSV.

The word for believe in Greek is *pisteuō*, meaning to think to be true, to be persuaded of, to give credit or place confidence in. The word for faith in Greek is *pistis*, meaning a conviction of the truth. A conviction of truth that Jesus is the Messiah and the source of our eternal salvation. A conviction that God is the Creator of everything, the Almighty, Alpha, and Omega.

I know that when I read the word conviction, my mind immediately goes to a negative connotation. I see conviction as a sentencing a judge gives in a court of law. The word that is used in Greek for this is *élenchos* (el-eng-khos), meaning "a proof, that by which a thing is proved and tested." Another use of this word in Greek for conviction is evidence or to be convinced. In a conviction, it is because the judge or panel is convinced through evidence and proof that the person standing on trial is guilty. That is generally how we use the word conviction today. However, these definitions of faith and belief speak to me in a different context.

To believe in Jesus is to be persuaded that He is who he says He is, to give credit that He was real, and to place confidence in Him. To have faith in Jesus doesn't mean just being persuaded that Jesus is King of Kings and Lord of Lords but being convinced without a shadow of a doubt. To believe in something through persuasion means that another persuasion can come in and take its place if we do not have faith in what we believe in. I can believe that what the Bible says is true because it is what I was brought up with and raised in. However, if I do not have faith in what I believe in, it is not set on solid ground, and a storm strong enough can shake it off its foundations.

Simply believing is not enough; this world and the enemy behind it can change the way we believe if we are not strong in our faith. If we do not know Jesus enough to know with full confidence in Him, then our faith is weak. That is why we have our shield of faith; our beliefs and walk with God are guarded by it. If our faith is strong, the arrows the enemy fires have much less of a chance of hitting us. Just like in the movies when the opposing army darkens the sky with their legion of arrows, the soldiers lift their shields to keep them safe. If we do not have a solid foundation in our beliefs rooted in strong faith, the strikes may become hard to defend and may penetrate through our armor.

Our Faith in Jesus is so much more than just armor and shield. It is the very essence of our being as a disciple of Jesus. In Matthew chapter four, Jesus tells us that we do not live on bread alone but by the Word of God. Jesus is telling us that we need Him just as much as we need food and drink to live. Jesus is the living Word of God, and He lives inside of us.

If we are only choosing to believe in Jesus because that is how we were raised to believe, then do we really have faith in Him? If we do not have full faith in Him, then our spirits and souls will be starved, always looking for more and often finding it in all the wrong places. Romans 10:17 tells us that "faith comes from hearing, and hearing through the word of Christ." NASB.m2 Corinthians 5:7 tells us "for we walk by faith and not by sight." NKJV. Psalm 119:105 tells us, "Thy word is a lamp unto my feet, and a light to my path." KJV.

This tells me that having faith is how we see, how we walk, and how we hear the voice of God. It is how we understand the plans and path that He has for us. If we do not have faith in what we believe, how do we expect others to follow and believe for themselves? How can we walk and lead others in the faith if we are just the blind leading the blind?

Hebrews 11:6 tells us, "And without faith, it is impossible to please him, for whoever would draw near to God must believe that he exists and that he rewards those who seek him." ESV. Being Christians means that we are to Jesus' disciples, spreading God's love through the Gospel and the good news of Jesus. This tells us that we must believe in God, draw near to Him, and seek His face. We must be willing, trusting, and believing with every beat of our hearts that He is Lord, and the reward is faith.

> "For by grace you have been saved through faith. And this is not your own doing; it is the gift of God, not a result of works, so that no one may boast" Ephesians 2:8-9 ESV.

It is by faith that we believe God created the universe by speaking it into existence. It was by faith that Enoch was taken into heaven so that he would see death. It was by faith that Moses climbed to the top of the mountain and met with God, forever changing the history of mankind. It was by faith that Peter got out of the boat and walked on water. It is by our faith that the impossible can become possible.

> "Faith is taking the first step even, when you don't see the whole staircase." -Martin Luther King Jr.

Just as important as realizing how much we need faith in our belief, we must put this faith into action. If we build this faith in Jesus so strong that it becomes unshakable but keep it to ourselves, then what purpose does it serve? We do not go to college or school to build our knowledge and skills to just keep them to ourselves. We become educated and skilled to build and shape the future of our communities and country. We do not need people to become engineers, architects, or scientists, only for them not to use their gifts and abilities.

Building our faith up in Jesus works in the same manner. We build it up to advance the Kingdom of Heaven. We grow and learn in our faith, becoming disciples, leaders, servants, preachers, and teachers helping to build up and advance the Kingdom of Heaven.

I have never really thought about it like that before. I know that putting our faith into action can be much easier said than done. I will be the first to admit that I have struggled in this more than I would like to say. Let me give you an example. When the Holy Spirit first spoke this book to me, it was many years ago. Almost eight years, to be exact. Admitting this on paper, knowing that it will be read by who knows how many people, almost brings shame over me.

Eight years ago, this book was birthed into my spirit with all the chapters and the thesis behind it. I was full of zeal and eagerness to write it, but I did not act on it. I never put the faith of writing into action. I want to be completely honest and raw with you right now. I would tell people for years that

I was writing a book while never putting a single word down on paper. I went to the store and bought a notepad for each chapter with the full intention of filling each page. All those notebooks are packed away somewhere in a box in the garage.

I never stepped into action, knowing that the calling of God was on my life and Him speaking through me as I have always prayed for was collecting dust in a box somewhere. I am almost in tears just writing about this. How could I let that happen? God spoke to my heart and told me that the door to ministry would open once the book was finished. But there I was, always talking about taking action while never moving a step forward.

I know that life gets busy, and we have jobs that take up most of our time. Some of us have families and children who take up the rest of it. We have hobbies and sports and our favorite shows that we love to keep up with. As I sit here and write this, I think to myself, "Why don't I sacrifice any of that to spend time with my King? Why don't I use some of that time to sacrifice some of my wants and desires to bring edification to the Kingdom of Heaven?"

James tells us in his second letter to the twelve tribes that faith without works is dead. He says that just as a body without a spirit is dead, so also faith without works is dead. It has been said that the meaning of faith without works is dead because the lack of works shows a spiritually dead or unchanged heart. Was I not putting my faith into action because of burnout? Or was it because I had become spiritually dead from my lack of works? Or is it because I had become a lazy Christian? Was I comfortable in the season that I was in?

When my wife and I were in the early stages of our relationship and falling deeper in love, we spent as much time as we could together, and then I worked the rest of it. Was it because I had gotten into a routine of an "ordinary" life? I had just spent a yearlong internship with my spiritual father, traveling from coast to coast almost every week, and slipped into a "break" from it that perhaps formed a routine that shaped an inactive walk in my faith. I know that I was not actively separating myself from this routine to spend quality time with God.

I would worship in my car to and from work, but I never sacrificed any time to get alone with Him and build my faith. I still believed in God, and life was good, but where were the works of my faith? Where was the walking in action? I firmly believe that it was my lack of Faith in action that has kept us in this season of waiting. The door that I had been praying and pleading for to open was waiting on me to get off my butt and get into action.

> "For this very reason, make every effort to supplement your faith with virtue, and virtue with knowledge, and knowledge with self-control, and self-control with steadfastness and

> steadfastness with godliness, and godliness with brotherly affection, and brotherly affection with love. For if these qualities are yours and are increasing, they keep you from being ineffective or unfruitful in the knowledge of our Lord Jesus Christ." 2 Peter 1:5-8 ESV

Man, I could just put that verse as the entire chapter here and end it with James 1:22—"Be doers of the word, and not just hearers only, deceiving yourselves." NKJV. That sums up this entire chapter in just a few sentences. Read that verse again from 2 Peter. Notice that it says to make every effort. Make every effort to supplement your faith.

The word supplement means something that completes or enhances something else when added to it, according to Oxford Languages. With this added definition, we can read it as "make every effort to enhance your faith." This is written in command form, so it is literally telling us to never stop growing and enhancing our faith. Our faith can never outgrow an all-consuming fire, so we must continually grow in our walk with God.

When it says works, that can pertain to how we walk and carry ourselves in Christ. It can be how we treat other people in this life. Or how we spend time with God. It can be how we walk in unwavering faith in this modern world that wants to snuff out

God's truth and replace it with a manmade one. Our works can be walking louder than how we talk. Being doers of the Word, not just hearers, can show love to those who feel unloved and looked down upon.

Sharing the love of Christ is the ultimate act of faith in action. I love what Mother Teresa said: "Faith in action is love, and love in action is service. By transforming that faith into living acts of love, we put ourselves in contact with God Himself, with Jesus our Lord." The ultimate act of faith in action is love—chasing the love of God, showing the loving God, sharing the love of God. I say this because "God so loved the world that He gave His only begotten Son, that whoever believes in him should not perish but have everlasting life" John 3:16 NKJV.

Jesus showed the greatest love by sacrificing Himself on that cross so that we could be saved by His grace and by our faith in Him. With this grace and love, our faith can stand the test of time, and even if we fall short (which we will), the seed of faith can never wither away. It may seem like it has, but all it needs is a drink of water from the well that will never run dry. Just as I let this book, this calling, this dream sit and sit and seem to wither away and be done with, all it took was getting back to the well and putting my faith into action.

If you are reading this and the Spirit is speaking to you right now, it is time to get back to the well and get an action plan. God is calling to His people to stand firm in faith now more than ever, to protect our children, to stand for truth, and to bring light into this dark world. The attacks against the Kingdom seem to be getting stronger and stronger. I am concerned that if we believe just to believe and not have faith, then we fall short of the glory of God, and we need the glory of God to shine bright. I am afraid that if we have faith and don't put any action behind it, then we will become spiritually dead Christians, raising more spiritually dead Christians.

Remember the ending of the verse in 2 Peter 1:5-8—"For if these qualities are yours and are increasing, they keep you from being ineffective or unfruitful in the knowledge of our Lord Jesus Christ"? I don't want to be an ineffective or unfruitful Christian. I have been one before, and I never want to go back there again. I want to get to Heaven knowing that I gave it my all and that I made every effort I could to put my faith into action. I don't want to get to heaven knowing that because of my lack, I left my bag of seeds full and not planted. Therefore not allowing the seeds to grow fruit for others to eat.

If this, too, is you, I urge you, as I urge myself, to create an action plan. Let's call it the "Faith in Action Plan." I am not kidding when I say I am making myself one. I think that this is an amazing idea, and the great thing about writing things down is we can come back to them later. Let's get a notebook and make an action plan of what we can start implementing today to put our faith into action. Things like setting aside time to get alone and spend time with God, skipping that TV show tonight and reading our Bibles, and thinking of ways to walk out our faith while at work.

Maybe you, too, have felt a call to write. Make a plan of when and how to get started. Get your notebook, get alone with God, and pray for guidance and wisdom on ways to put faith into action.

If we find ourselves getting back to a lack of action, we can pull it out and make the effort to enhance our faith again. I know that life can get busy, trust me I really do understand. However, if making small sacrifices, or large ones, enhances and supplements our faith so that we won't be ineffective, those sacrifices seem worth it to me. There is success in sacrifice, and I am learning that myself as well. I know that we can do this; I know that you can do this. If God is for us, who can be against us? The Bible tells us that we are more than conquerors through Christ who loves us (Romans 8:31-39). I believe in you!

Pray with me,

"Heavenly Father, I come boldly to your throne right now. Thank you for the opportunity to grow in my faith. Thank you, Lord, that you are full of love and grace, for I need it every day of my life. Father, if I have had unbelief in my heart or the lack of it that has kept me from

having and keeping faith in you, forgive me and lead me to your well. I want to know you better; I want to sit at your feet and drink from the cup in your hand. I want to have faith in action so that I can grow and enhance my walk with you so that your love and light will shine through me and into others. I want to live in your purpose and in your will for my life. Show me and teach me to seek your face and the things needed to fulfill your Word so that I may be a worker in your field to bring the harvest. Jesus, if my seed of faith has gone dry, all I need is a drink from your well. One sip and everything can change. Thank you, Jesus, for your living water. I can feel your waters flowing into me now. Thank you. Let it grow and let it show everywhere that I go. In the name of Jesus I pray, amen."

Even if life gets busy and it may seem impossible to make the time, remember that there is success in sacrifice. A seed must sacrifice its protective coating by breaking open for it to take root and grow.

Conclusion

I pray that reading this book has been the same experience as it has been for me writing it: a breath of fresh air, a fresh anointing, and an awakening of your spirit. I pray that we take everything we have read and received from this and apply it all to our daily lives.

In the last chapter, we talked about putting our faith into action and that the Bible tells us to make every effort to supplement our faith. We also read that the Bible teaches us that faith without works is dead. Another way that we can grow our faith and put it to work is by being a servant of Christ. Whether that be serving in your church, an outreach, or in a soup kitchen feeding the hungry, we all should be serving somehow to better serve the Kingdom.

In Matthew 20:26-28 Jesus tells us, "But among you, it will be different. Whoever wants to be a leader among you must be your servant, and whoever wants to be first among you must become your slave. For even the Son of Man came not to be served but to serve others and to give his life as a ransom for many." NLT.

Jesus said that He did not come to be served but to serve. Think about that for a minute. The incarnate Word of God came to serve the people over whom He has all authority. He did not come to be served. That is so powerful, and we learn a lot from this about having a servant's heart mentality. If Jesus, the Son of God and Word made flesh, came to this earth to serve His people and sacrifice His life as a ransom for the multitudes, why should we not be serving as much as we can?

As a member of the body of Christ and as leaders of the body—especially pastors, teachers, and elders—it is our duty to accept leadership to be the greatest servants we can be. I have said so many times that the greatest leaders come from being the greatest servants. Jesus is the greatest role model of leadership that there has ever been, and yet He was the greatest servant. A servant to the will of His Father, a servant to His disciples by the washing of their feet.

That was a job created for the servants of the house to do. It was a dirty and stinky job, and yet the Son of God knelt to His knees to wash their feet. How incredible is that? He probably could have commanded the water to wash them itself, becoming the first washing machine, but He lowered himself into the position of servant and slave. What a beautiful picture of love and sacrifice Jesus shows us.

We must become the best servants that we can be to the Kingdom, following Jesus' lead, knowing that showing the greatest act of leadership we can is one of love. It is being eye to eye with others, not acting or showing superiority, but lowering ourselves and being willing to dirty up our knees to put our faith into action.

From the front of this book to the end, I hope and pray that the Holy Spirit has spoken to you as much as He has to me. I pray that you have been given new revelations and a new hunger for Christ. A new thirst for His Word like never before. I can see now that every word in this book, spoken by the Holy Spirit through me, was written for me just as much as it is for anyone else.

Writing this has changed the trajectory of my life and my outlook on things. It has opened my eyes and my heart again. I have been listening to a worship song by Housefires on repeat recently. In the song, they are asking Jesus to reintroduce Himself to them like making an old friend into a new one again. This book has done just that for me, and I am so thankful that God has still entrusted and kept this book for me to write. Putting my faith into action and tackling this book head-on has led to seeking a deeper, genuine, and authentic relationship with my Savior. I hope and pray that it has for you, too.

I must do one last word study for you before ending this. What do I mean by genuine Christianity? Or being an authentic Christian? I think that sometimes, we seek productivity over authenticity in the church. I believe that in today's Christian world, we have put more focus on the productivity of the church over the authenticity of it.

We put in so much work to produce more views, followers and likes. I believe that we, as disciples of Jesus, should not live a performance-style life for maximum productivity but to live our lives with a pursuit of maximum authenticity. The Bible tells us to seek yet His Kingdom first, and then all else will be added. I think that we have lost our grasp on this, to where we perform so that the productivity will be maximized to try and bring in more people.

I believe that if we strive to be as authentic as we can with our walk with Jesus, He will do the rest. God does not call for perfection but pursuit! Authentic means to be genuine, being actually and exactly what is claimed. Authenticity in the form of art is described as how individuals experience art as being authentic, real, or original as opposed to being commercial or made for profit.

I use that definition in the form of art because the Bible tells us that we are the clay in the Potter's hands and that we are His masterpiece. He has crafted us to perfection. I fear, though, that the modern-day church has become commercialized and slipped into a slippery slope with the mainstream and worldly connection. We are called to be separated from the secularistic ways of this world, but we have grown into a comfortable place where we chase maximum production to please man while saying it is all for God. We paint a good picture of Jesus, but it is just the outline. For us to truly please our Father and live as He has designed us to be, we need to focus our attention and gaze toward the pursuit of authenticity in our walk and relationship with Jesus.

In this book, we have learned the magnitude of how important it is to know who we are in Christ and whose we are in Christ. Our identity in Him is of crucial importance in our identity of being a Christian and not becoming conformed to this world but being set apart from it.

We have learned the importance of God's Word and how it is the lifeline to our veins. How it is our very being in Jesus, and the consequences of not being in the Word of God. We have learned what it means to truly repent, to chase righteousness and the unctioning of the Holy Spirit. We must keep a constant and conscious choice to guard our hearts and minds of what we let in. What goes in does, in fact, come out. We have learned that we must continuously battle for our minds. How we walk and talk is a direct reflection of who we are in Christ, and when we are not full of Him, it affects how we treat others.

In the chapter "Where is the Love?" we saw the importance of having a Christlike love for others. There is no greater act than the act of love and imitating Christ in our attitude. We learned about becoming broken before the Lord and the glory that it brings to the Father when we are. We have learned how putting our faith into action is one of the most crucial parts of our walk with Christ. Remember, we do not want to become ineffective or unfruitful for the Kingdom of Heaven. I believe that if we take all these things we have read and learned throughout this journey and by keeping God in reverence, then we can walk, live, and operate from a place of authenticity and oneness with Christ.

As we discussed in the intro to this book, Compromised Christianity can be defined as a half-measured Christian. The Bible tells us not to be lukewarm, or we will be spit out of the mouth of God. We cannot straddle both sides of the fence between worldliness and godliness. We must choose one or the other. We cannot serve two masters, so we must choose who we are serving. Are we serving ourselves? Are we serving the principalities and rulers of this world? Or are we going to serve the one true King, our Lord and Savior, Jesus Christ?

Pray with me one last time.

"Heavenly Father, thank you so much for this journey that you have taken me on. Thank you for the growth and the shifting in my spirit and relationship with you. Open up my heart to let all

these words sink in and keep a place within. Just like your Word tells us to hide your scriptures in our hearts, hide them within me now. Teach me and guide me, give me the burning passion to make every effort to enhance and build my relationship deeper with you continually. Give me a never-ending thirst and hunger for more of you. I want to walk in authentic and genuine faith so that you can use me as the vessel that you have created me to be. Give me the steadfastness to persevere through this life and never take my sights off you. I do not want to be an unfruitful or half-measured Christian; I want the fullness of you so that I can spread your love everywhere I go. Thank you for your love, thank you for your grace, thank you for your mercy, and thank you for your sacrifice on the cross. Walk with me all the days of my life and let me walk along beside you. In Jesus' mighty name, amen."

Now, I want to pray with you as an appreciation for going on this journey with me. Just a few more moments, I promise. A good pastor always has ten closings.

"Dear Heavenly Father, thank you so much for this child of yours. Thank you for allowing them to be a part of this journey with me. Thank you for entrusting me with writing this book, breathed by your Holy Spirit, to lead this wonderful child of yours towards a new journey of life. I pray that you, Jesus, have touched

them for life and ignited a new fire within. A fire bigger and brighter than any past flames. I pray for a fresh and new anointing to flow over right now in Jesus' name. I declare a hedge of protection over this child of yours and the Holy Spirit's guidance as we begin to walk in this new anointing. The attacks from the enemy may come, but we are well-equipped to go into any battle. For this battle is yours and is already won. I pray that every word in this book has been a breath of fresh air and fills the lungs anew. Lord, walk with this child, son or daughter, and let them chase you more than ever before. Just as you have transformed my life, transform theirs. Thank you again, Lord, for all that you have done during this time of reading together. And thank you for all that is to come. The best days of our lives are ahead of us. I pray all of these things in Jesus' name, amen."

"Audacious faith is the raw material that authentic Christianity is made of. It's the stuff that triggers ordinarily level-headed people like you and me to start living with unusual boldness."
-Pastor Steven Furtick

1 Timothy 4 NLT

Now the Holy Spirit tells us clearly that in the last times some will turn away from the true faith; they will follow deceptive spirits and teachings that come from demons. These people are hypocrites and liars, and their consciences are dead.

They will say it is wrong to be married and wrong to eat certain foods. But God created those foods to be eaten with thanks by faithful people who know the truth. Since everything God created is good, we should not reject any of it but receive it with thanks. For we know it is made acceptable by the word of God and prayer.

If you explain these things to the brothers and sisters, Timothy, you will be a worthy servant of Christ Jesus, one who is nourished by the message of faith and the good teaching you have followed. Do not waste time arguing over godless ideas and old wives' tales. **Instead, train yourself to be godly. "Physical training is good, but training for godliness is much better, promising benefits in this life and in the life to come."** This is a trustworthy saying, and everyone should accept it. This is why we work hard and continue to struggle, for our hope is in the living God, who is the Savior of all people and particularly of all believers.

Teach these things and insist that everyone learn them. Don't let anyone think less of you because you are young. **Be an example to all believers in what you say, in the way you live, in your love, your faith, and your purity.** Until I get there, focus on reading the Scriptures to the church, encouraging the believers, and teaching them.

Do not neglect the spiritual gift you received through the prophecy spoken over you when the elders of the church laid their hands on you. Give your complete attention to these matters. Throw yourself into your tasks so that everyone will see your progress. **Keep a close watch on how you live** and on your teaching. Stay true to what is right for the sake of your own salvation and the salvation of those who hear you.

About the Author

Michael is from Pinson, Alabama born and raised. Michael gave his heart to the Lord when he was thirteen years old but got caught up with the wrong crowd in his high school years and began to fall away from God. This led him to live a life of addiction for several years until he admitted himself to a Christian rehab and got his life back on track with God.

With a renewed heart and mind, he was blessed to attend a ministry internship where he was able to travel from coast to coast. He traveled with his spiritual father, Pat Schatzline, who wrote the foreword for this book. He has seen tens of thousands of lives changed, from the scars of teens cutting themselves disappearing to adults being radically set free from a lifetime of sin. Michael has bore witness to the radical encounters of God that have marked him by Heaven for life.

In completing this internship, he received a certificate of ministry. He also met his wife Sydni as they served together in this ministry. Whom he married in March of 2017. Michael and Sydni now live in Northeast Tennessee with their beautiful daughter Aria. He has a heart and calling for full-time ministry and a passion to see the Lost and Hurting come to know Jesus personally and be set free for life.

If you would like to contact the author for scheduling or questions, please email Michael at **compromisedchristianbook@gmail.com.**

Notes

Introduction

1. https://www.elevateddiscourse.com/single-post/2020/09/01/tuesday-september-1st-2020

2. https://translate.google.com/details?sl=auto&tl=iw&text=compromise&op=translate&hl=en

Chapter 1. The Conformed Christian

1. https://translate.google.com/details?sl=auto&tl=iw&text=compromise&op=translate&hl=en

2. https://www.merriam-webster.com/dictionary/conform

3. https://dictionary.cambridge.org/us/dictionary/english/compromise

4. https://dictionary.cambridge.org/us/dictionary/english/perception

5. https://dictionary.cambridge.org/us/dictionary/english/deceive

6. https://www.merriam-webster.com/dictionary/deceived

7. https://www.wordhippo.com/what-is/the/hebrew-word-for-a001cafb5791b83353005de6ad21783ec2c63155.html

8. https://www.merriam-webster.com/dictionary/identity

9. https://www.wordhippo.com/what-is/the/hebrew-word-for-1db089a9f84e14e95f11dcb5c57fa10d60aa84bb.html

10. https://www.merriam-webster.com/dictionary/crisis

11. https://www.merriam-webster.com/dictionary/paroxysm#word-history

12. https://www.azquotes.com/author/22943-Howard_G_Hendricks?p=2

13. *Howard G. Hendricks, William D. Hendricks (2007). "Living By the Book/Living By the Book Workbook Set", p.6, Moody Publishers*

14. *J.C. Ryle (2015). "Holiness: It's Nature, Hindrances, Difficulties, and Roots", p.257, Letcetera Publishing*

Chapter 2. Walking Without God's Word & Living Apart from It

1. https://www.azquotes.com/quotes/topics/word-of-god.html
2. https://www.ashevillenc.gov/news/wellness-wednesday-cultural-appreciation-can-help-you-understand-yourself-better/
3. https://www.susanldavis.com/how-does-reading-the-bible-affect-your-brain/
4. https://www.christianitytoday.com/news/2021/may/bible-reading-study-trauma-ptsd-covid19-mental-health.html
5. https://www.christianitytoday.com/news/2021/may/bible-reading-study-trauma-ptsd-covid19-mental-health.html
6. Switch on your brain. Dr Caroline Leaf. Baker Books (2015)
7. https://openthebible.org/article/what-happens-when-you-dont-read-your-bible/

8. https://charismamag.com/widget/

9. https://pastorbaker.blog/2014/03/18/31714-the-powerful-word-of-god/

10. Smith Wigglesworth quote: https://www.azquotes.com/quote/522677

11. https://pastorbaker.blog/2012/08/28/82712-having-a-heart-on-fire-for-god/

12. https://www.blueletterbible.org/lexicon/h7878/kjv/wlc/0-1/

13. Davis, Andrew. 2003. Holes. United States: Buena Vista Pictures

Chapter 3. Where is the love?

1. https://dictionary.cambridge.org/us/dictionary/english/compassion

2. Azquotes.com

3. *Elizabeth George (2013). "Moments of Grace for a Woman's Heart", p.110 , Harvest House Publishers*

4. Black Eyed Peas. (2004). Where is the love? In Elephunk [CD]. New York, NY: A&M Records, Inc.

5. *Where There Is Love, There Is God: A Path to Closer Union with God and Greater Love for Others".*

6. *Jamie Tworkowski (2015). "If You Feel Too Much DELUXE: Thoughts on Things Found and Lost and Hoped For", p.82, Penguin*

7. *Dalai Lama, Victor Chan (2012). "The Wisdom of Compassion: Stories of Remarkable Encounters and Timeless Insights", p.11, Random House*

8. Martin Luther King, Jr. *Martin Luther King Jr. (1963). "Strength to Love"*

9. https://www.merriam-webster.com/dictionary/compassion

10. https://ratiochristi.org/blog/words-for-love-in-the-bible/?gclid=CjwKCAiAxP2eBhBiEiwA5puhNX4CJhH_7FVGGdPLTg75QhexSTMsIHAYdzKmshY3tPBghd6Wrw7UwxoCSYAQAvD_BwE

11. *https://hebrew.jerusalemprayerteam.org/mercy-compassion-womb/* also see *https://biblehub.com/hebrew/7356.htm*

Chapter 4. We Are Unbroken

1. *Smith Wigglesworth (2013). "The Teachings of Smith Wigglesworth", p .101, Simon and Schuster*

2. https://dictionary.cambridge.org/us/dictionary/english/brokenness

3. https://e360bible.org/blog/the-meaning-of-brokenness-truth-about-being-broken-in-the-sight-of-god/

4. https://www.goodreads.com/quotes/97169-god-uses-broken-things-it-takes-broken-soil-to-produce

5. *The More I Seek You (2006).* Integrity Music. Zach Neese. Kari Jobe. mtID: 84

6. David Wilkerson- a call to anguish -https://www.sermonindex.net/modules/articles/index.php?aid=32622&view=article

7. https://www.merriam-webster.com/dictionary/bend

8. https://www.desiringgod.org/articles/agony-in-the-garden

9. https://www.webmd.com/a-to-z-guides/hematidrosis-hematohidrosis

10. https://walesawakening.org/revivalhistory/The-Bending-at-Blaenannerch.pdf

11. https://www.revival-library.org/revival_histories/evangelical/1900/welsh_revival_1904.shtml

Chapter 5. Life without repentance

1. The Teachings of Ezra Taft Benson (ed. Bookcraft Pubs, 1988)

2. https://www.merriam-webster.com/dictionary/repentance

3. *John Ortberg (2008). "When the Game Is Over, It All Goes Back in the Box", p.121, Zondervan*

4. https://godtv.com/meaning-of-the-hebrew-word-of-repent/

5. https://www.crosswalk.com/faith/bible-study/what-is-the-meaning-of-metanoia-and-its-biblical-significance.html

6. https://www.merriam-webster.com/dictionary/apology

7. https://www.merriam-webster.com/dictionary/apologia#little-gems

Chapter 6. Righteousness over religion

1. https://www.blueletterbible.org/lexicon/h6663/kjv/wlc/0-1/
2. https://activechristianity.org/29-eye-opening-bible-verses-about-righteousness
3. https://www.houmatoday.com/story/lifestyle/faith/2017/08/11/by-his-grace-to-live-righteous-life-is-to-walk-with-christ/19804544007/#
4. https://www.thegospelcoalition.org/blogs/erik-raymond/what-is-the-difference-between-justification-and-sanctification/?amp
5. https://www.merriam-webster.com/dictionary/righteous
6. https://dictionary.cambridge.org/us/dictionary/english/righteous
7. https://www.brainyquote.com/quotes/johann_arndt_227143?src=t_righteousness
8. https://www.pewresearch.org/religion/2011/12/19/global-christianity-exec/
9. https://goodfaithmedia.org/global-christia

n-population-projected-to-reach-3-3-billion-by-2050/

10. https://www.christiancentury.org/blogs/archive/2013-09/being-religious

11. https://www.britannica.com/topic/Greek-religion

12. https://ulpan.com/how-to-say-religion-in-hebrew

13. https://timeofreckoning.org/category/hebrew-word-for-religion

14. https://www.christianity.com/wiki/christian-terms/what-is-legalism-definition-and-examples.html#google_vignette

15. https://www.livingwordchapel.org/bible-study-notes/righteousness-the-basis-of-it-all/

16. https://seminary.grace.edu/what-is-sanctification/

17. https://www.blueletterbible.org/lexicon/h6942/kjv/wlc/0-1/

Chapter 7. Where is the Unction?

1. Why Revival Tarries- Leonard Ravenhill.

Bethany House Publisher (2004)

2. https://kingjamesbibledictionary.com/Dictionary/unction

3. https://biblehub.com/greek/5545.htm

4. https://www.lwf.org/sermons/audio/how-to-function-with-unction-1968

Chapter 8. An Unguarded Heart

1. https://www.azquotes.com/author/19456-K_P_Yohannan?p=2

2. https://www.grahampsychology.com.au/blog/the-power-of-music#:~:text=Research%20findings%20have%20demonstrated%20that,even%20help%20us%20sleep%20better.

3. *https://www.psychologytoday.com/us/blog/peacemeal/201301/what-happens-if-you-dont-watch-what-you-watch#:~:text=It%20turns%20out%20that%20what,for%20your%20mind%20and%20soul*
.

4. https://www.hopkinsmedicine.org/health/wellness-and-prevention/keep-your-brain-young-with-music

5. *https://hebrewwordlessons.com/2019/02/10/lev-the-heart-of-who-you-are/*

6. *https://bibleproject.com/explore/video/lev-heart/#:~:text=We're%20going%20to%20look,in%20a%20shorter%20form%20lev.*

7. *Reference: David Wilkerson-A Call to Anguish - https://www.sermonindex.net/modules/articles/index.php?aid=32622&view=article*

8. https://drleaf.com/blogs/news/what-is-the-mind

9. Switch on your brain. Dr Caroline Leaf. Baker Books (2015)

Chapter 9. Relevance Over Reverence

1. https://www.azquotes.com/quote/1125431?ref=reverence

2. https://dictionary.cambridge.org/us/dictionary/english/relevance

3. https://www.merriam-webster.com/dictionary/reverence

4. Dickson, Terry. "Inalienable Sayings That Are Out There." Florida Times Union, vol. , no. , 2014, p. B.1.

5. https://www.collinsdictionary.com/us/dictionary/english/obeisance

6. https://www.dictionary.com/browse/fear

7. https://www.dictionary.com/browse/awe

8. https://webstersdictionary1828.com/Dictionary/fear

Chapter 10. Belief without faith, Faith without action

1. https://christianfaithguide.com/how-many-times-is-faith-mentioned-in-the-bible/

2. https://www.christianbiblereference.org/faq_WordCount.htm

3. https://www.blueletterbible.org/lexicon/g4100/kjv/tr/0-1/

4. https://www.blueletterbible.org/lexicon/g4102/kjv/tr/0-1/

5. https://biblehub.com/greek/1650.htm

6. https://www.openbible.info/topics/faith

7. https://www.brainyquote.com/quotes/martin_luther_king_jr_105087, accessed December 7, 2023.

8. https://www.gotquestions.org/faith-without-works-dead.html

9. https://www.bibleref.com/James/2/James-2-26.html

10. https://www.google.com/search?q=supplement

11. https://www.merriam-webster.com/dictionary/supplement

Conclusion

1. https://www.merriam-webster.com/dictionary/authentic

2. https://dictionary.cambridge.org/us/dictionary/english/authentic

3. https://www.azquotes.com/author/19553-Steven_Furtick

www.ingramcontent.com/pod-product-compliance
Lightning Source LLC
LaVergne TN
LVHW051056080426
835508LV00019B/1901

* 9 7 9 8 9 9 0 4 1 4 4 0 2 *